The Mémoire Justificatif of the Chevalier Montault de Monberaut

THE

MEMOIRE JUSTIFICATIF

OF THE CHEVALIER MONTAULT DE MONBERAUT

Indian Diplomacy in British West Florida, 1763-1765

TRANSLATION AND INTRODUCTION BY

MILO B. HOWARD, JR.

AND

ROBERT R. REA

UNIVERSITY OF ALABAMA PRESS

Tuscaloosa

Southern Historical Publications No. 3

Library of Congress Catalog Card Number: 64-24955
ISBN 0-8173-5051-9 (alk. paper)

Contents

Foreword

HISTORIANS OF THE Gulf Coast have long delighted in the romance of Spanish discovery and French settlement. The period of British occupation was relatively brief, fruitless, and prosaic, if we are to believe the older authorities. Today the availability of materials which were closed to an earlier generation enables us to re-create the story of British West Florida in terms more precise, with details more personal, and with no less dramatic coloration than has long been given—with less accuracy—to the earlier epochs.

In this volume we have undertaken the resurrection of one of those gallant Frenchmen of the *ancien régime* who remained behind to serve the new Anglo-Saxon masters of West Florida. The Chevalier Montault de Monberaut is not unknown to historians of the colonial scene, but he has never enjoyed a full portrayal of his contribution nor a balanced evaluation of his role. By concentrating our attention upon the man as well as his milieu, we have been able to present in greater detail than before the circumstances and procedure of Indian diplomacy on the Gulf Coast at the beginning of the British period. By placing Monberaut against the backdrop of British colonial government and its problems, we have replaced some of the romantic fallacies with historic realities. The resulting clarity adds to the picture's significance and appeal.

In order to allow the reader to catch the *esprit* of the *Mémoire* we have translated Monberaut's French into English as faithfully as possible, taking a hand only to systematize the variety of his spelling and reining in his Gallic fluency only where necessary. As the style of his English and Scottish correspondents has been preserved, so have we attempted to retain Monberaut's.

It is impossible to approach the subject of American colonial history, and particularly that of British West Florida, without obeisance to the great manuscript collection of the William L. Clements Library, Ann Arbor, Michigan. The bulk of the literary remains of Montault de Monberaut are to be found there among the papers of General Thomas Gage. It is our very real pleasure to express our warmest gratitude to Howard H. Peckham, Director of the William L. Clements Library, and to his staff, for permission to use and to reproduce material in the Gage Papers. Dr. Peckham's interest and encouragement has extended well beyond the limits of this volume; we avow our personal obligations also.

We are deeply appreciative of the assistance rendered by our several colleagues and the cooperative officials of a number of institutions: the Library of Congress Manuscripts Division, Washington, D.C.; the Archives de France, Paris; and the Auburn University Library. Unpublished Crown Copyright material in the Public Record Office, London, has been reproduced by permission of the Controller of Her Majesty's Stationery Office. We are indebted in many ways to Mr. Peter A. Brannon of the State Department of Archives and History, Montgomery, whose knowledge and interest regarding the Indians of this region has been of aid and inspiration. Assistance of a tangible nature has been provided by Auburn University through a series of research grants-in-aid.

To know M. de Monberaut is not—necessarily—to love him. We have marched with him through the wilderness, confronted thousands of howling redskins, endured his pangs of injured honor and recorded his endless declarations of probity and sincerity; we have, as did his British colleagues, found him to be a typical Frenchman in all things save one: *pointe des femmes!* In order that we may avoid the charge of incredibility, whatever else may be our lot, we wish herewith to provide Monberaut's book with that which we could not give him, and so we dedicate this volume to *les femmes que nous aimons et qui nous aiment.*

Auburn and Montgomery, Alabama Milo B. Howard, Jr.
Charlottesville, Virginia Robert R. Rea

Introduction

The Coming of the British

The Great War for Empire, known to most Americans as the French and Indian War, marked the culminating triumph of British arms in the New World. From the Plains of Abraham to the walls of Morro Castle, the standards of the allied Bourbon powers, France and Spain, were lowered in defeat. The Peace of Paris, 1763, ratified the preponderance of Great Britain in North America and, supplemented by a concurrent Franco-Spanish agreement, it vastly altered the map of *l'Amérique Septentrionale.* France ceded to the English Canada and all Louisiana east of the Mississippi River, save the Isle of Orleans; Spain surrendered Florida but gained New Orleans and the western part of Louisiana in easement of that loss. Thus, at one blow, the extent of the British Empire in North America more than doubled, and the burden of imperial administration increased proportionately.

While contending with the rising tide of independence in the older colonies, the British government confronted other problems in the newly acquired territories which demanded prompt attention. Colonial governments had to be established which would encourage British immigration and at the same time satisfy the settled alien populace, and Indian policy had to be devised whereby the friendship of the Francophile natives might be won and kept. The critical nature of Indian relations became alarmingly evident as that bloody rising known as Pontiac's Conspiracy threatened to spread fire and massacre along the whole frontier. These problems assumed their own peculiar shape in the formerly half-French, half-Spanish province of West Florida.[1]

British West Florida sprawled along the Gulf Coast from the Apalachicola River west to the Iberville, Lake Pontchartrain, and the Mississippi, thereby including parts of both the French and Spanish cessions. Its northern boundary, established on the thirty-first parallel and later drawn from the mouth of the Yazoo River, was lost in the forests of Indian country as yet known to but a few daring English traders. French Mobile and Spanish Pensacola, the only towns deserving of the name, were now reduced to waiting humbly for the conquering redcoat to appear. The withdrawal of the Spaniards and their Indian dependents from Pensacola[2] relieved the British of one disturbing element, but the French were more reluctant to depart. Established for half a century along the coast, they had enjoyed notable success in attaching the Choctaw Nation and many of the Creeks to their interest. The friendship of these tribes whose lands encircled the former French settlements was necessary to the very existence of the infant British province.

In the summer of 1763, British troops in Havana were ordered to take possession of West Florida. Lieutenant Colonel Augustine Prevost was dispatched to Pensacola with part of the 60th or Royal American Regiment, and Major Robert Farmar embarked the 22nd and 34th Regiments for transport to Mobile. The former post was occupied in August, the latter in October. Neither commander was prepared to negotiate with the Indians, but both were faced with that necessity.[3]

Within a few days of his occupation of Pensacola, Colonel Prevost was visited by more than 200 Indians representing five different Nations. Having no presents to give them, Prevost warmed them to their new masters with a little rum and many promises of

[1] See Lawrence Henry Gipson, *The Triumphant Empire: The British Empire Before the American Revolution* (New York, 1956), X.

[2] Wilbur H. Siebert, "How the Spaniards Evacuated Pensacola in 1763," *Florida Historical Quarterly*, XI (1932), 48-57.

[3] Clinton N. Howard, "The Military Occupation of British West Florida," *Florida Historical Quarterly*, XVII (1938-39), 181-197; and *The British Development of West Florida 1763-1769* (Berkeley, 1947), chap. iii.

fair treatment yet to come.[4] Toward the end of the year Creek chieftains, representing an estimated 6,000 braves, arrived at Pensacola and claimed all the lands around the fort as part of their hunting ground. Wolf King, the principal chief present, warned that the English might have only that land lying under the guns of the fort, which was all that the Creeks had ceded to the Spanish. Any attempt to encroach upon their territory, he declared, would be resisted by his warlike tribe.[5]

Major William Forbes, who succeeded Prevost in command, realized that without additional land Pensacola could not support a growing population and would, in fact, be hard put to provide sufficient food to sustain the garrison.[6] More land had to be obtained from the savages, but negotiations for such purposes were forbidden except at official congresses with the Indian chieftains. Private land speculation, which had started two months before Prevost's arrival, caused unrest among the natives and provided a further inducement for calling a conference. Consequently, a number of the leading Creek chiefs were invited to meet at Pensacola in September 1764. Major Forbes had been relieved by that date, and Captain Robert Mackinnen, the senior officer present, conducted the negotiations. Mackinnen was successful in winning some small territorial concessions from the Creeks, but his arrangements were soon abrogated on the grounds that he had exceeded his authority and the Indian signatories represented but a portion of the Creek Nation.[7] Nothing was gained by this abortive congress except the animosity of the chieftains who failed to attend, foremost among whom was The Mortar.[8] This was to prove a

[4] Letter from Augustine Prevost to the Secretary at War, September 7, 1763. Dunbar Rowland (ed.), *Mississippi Provincial Archives, 1763-1766. English Dominion* (Nashville, 1911), I, 136-137. Hereafter cited as *MPAED.*

[5] William Forbes's Report, January 30, 1764, and letter from Forbes to the Secretary of State, January 29, 1764, *ibid.*, I, 114, 142 f.

[6] *Ibid.*, I, 113-114.

[7] Mackinnen to Gage, September 20, 1764; Stuart to Gage, October 12, 1764, Gage Papers, William L. Clements Library, University of Michigan, Ann Arbor, Mich. Hereafter cited as Gage Papers.

[8] Yahatatastonake, known to the French as Le Loup, The Wolf, not to be confused with the Lower Creek Chief Wolf King who signed the Mackinnen Treaty at Pensacola in September, 1764.

stumbling block in the next congress, but most immediately it provided an additional irritant to the strained relations between Mackinnen and the newly-arrived governor, George Johnstone,[9] both speedily embroiled in controversy over the rival claims of civil and military authority.

If Governor Johnstone was displeased with the state of affairs at Pensacola, he was no better satisfied with conditions at Mobile. Major Robert Farmar[10] had taken possession of that town on October 20, 1763. The arrival of the British troops chanced to coincide with that of a large contingent of Choctaws who had been summoned to Mobile by the French. Despite the advice of French officials, Major Farmar promptly debarked his troops (which had been aboard ship for six weeks with only a brief respite at Pensacola) and ambitiously tackled the tasks at hand.[11] First, he issued a proclamation regulating the means whereby French habitants might secure their personal possessions under the British crown prior to becoming subjects or withdrawing from the province.[12] Then he turned his attention to the Indians whose good will was so necessary. Whether independently hostile or acting in conjunction with Pontiac, they threatened the position of the British in Mobile. On the other hand, if pacified, they might be induced to aid Farmar in carrying out his orders from General Thomas Gage[13] to

[9] George Johnstone (1730-87) enjoyed an undistinguished career in the Royal Navy, rising to the rank of commodore, before his appointment to the West Florida governorship. Recalled in 1767 after a stormy tenure of office, Johnstone entered parliament, served badly on the Eden mission to America in 1778, and subsequently returned to sea duty. He was notorious for his bad temper and haughty ways.

[10] Robert Farmar, Major of the 34th Regiment, commanded British forces occupying Mobile and subsequently led a detachment up the Mississippi to Fort Chartres. His quarrels with Governor Johnstone and his fellow officers in West Florida led to a court-martial which effectively cleared him, but he resigned his commission and later became one of Mobile's leading figures and landholders; elected to the General Assembly, Farmar remained in West Florida until its capture by the Spaniards in 1781.

[11] Farmar to the Secretary at War, January 24, 1764, *MPAED,* I, 10 f.

[12] Farmar's manifesto of October 20, 1763, *ibid.,* I, 60-63; see also D. C. McMurtrie, *A Broadside Issued at Mobile* (Privately printed, 1939).

[13] Thomas Gage (1721-87) served in America under Braddock and Amherst; commander-in-chief in America 1763-72; governor of Massachusetts 1774-75; his attempt to seize military stores at Concord precipitated the

proceed up the Mississippi River and occupy the forts of the Illinois country. The commander-in-chief was persuaded that the sooner French garrisons were replaced by British troops, the easier it would be to subdue the Indians and establish British rule throughout the western lands.[14]

With his problems painfully apparent, but with no instructions regarding Indian policy, Major Farmar was necessarily governed by the exigencies of the moment. The ruinous condition of Fort Charlotte—the new name he gave Fort Condé at Mobile—rendered it untenable by the fever-ridden and depleted British force. The presence of some three thousand savages, displeased with both the French and English for completing the transfer of Mobile without treating first with them, compelled Farmar to make promises which otherwise he might not have considered. The French practice of giving food and drink to the Indians was costly and, to Farmar, disagreeable, but he had to disregard his personal inclinations, as well as the economy so much desired by the ministry, and offer to continue all French customs.[15]

While the Choctaws were thus placated, the Creeks were reported to be preparing to join with the northern tribes in war against the English. Fort Tombecbe was occupied without incident, but Farmar determined against garrisoning Fort Toulouse in order to avoid further aggravations.[16] Hostile Indians thwarted all his efforts to ascend the Mississippi. Nonetheless, Major Farmar succeeded in keeping the Indians quiet in the environs of Mobile and even planned to push his luck to the point of holding a second congress with the Choctaws and Chickasaws in an effort to win their assistance in gaining access to the Illinois posts.[17]

American Revolution. See John R. Alden, *General Gage in America* (Baton Rouge, 1948).

[14] Gage to Farmar, May 20, 1764, Gage Papers.

[15] Farmar to Gage, March 29, April 3, April 17, 1764, Gage Papers. Farmar to the Secretary at War, January 24, 1764, *MPAED*, I, 7 ff.

[16] Farmar to the Secretary at War, January 24, 1764, *ibid.*, I, 12.

[17] John R. Alden, *John Stuart and the Southern Colonial Frontier* (Ann Arbor, 1944), pp. 195-196.

Farmar was not alone in estimating the friendship of the savages as highly important. General Gage, fully aware of the need for maintaining peaceful relations with the Indians of West Florida, instructed his subordinates to correspond with John Stuart, Superintendent of Indian Affairs for the southern colonies,[18] and to be guided by that gentleman's advice. Stuart preferred to appoint his own agents, and realizing that the military were having no success in doubling as diplomats, Gage agreed to yield direct control of the Indians to the superintendent, whom he urged to go in person to West Florida. Arriving at Pensacola in October 1764, Stuart found instructions from London to station himself in one of the Floridas and to appoint a deputy to reside in the other. He was to follow Gage's advice in choosing a base of operation, but the commander-in-chief, while recommending Pensacola, left the final choice to Stuart.[19]

John Stuart's appearance at Pensacola coincided with that of Governor George Johnstone, who had remained in England for nearly a year after his appointment. While still in England the governor had learned of the critical state of Indian affairs, and personal inspection substantiated every rumor.[20] The Choctaws were sulking because they felt neglected; the Creeks were thought to be plotting an attack upon the settlements; the boundary line between the Indian Nations and West Florida was as yet undetermined; and the expedition to the Illinois had met with utter failure.

In a thoroughly discouraging situation, one hope was offered to the harassed British officials. Still resident in the colony was the Chevalier Montault de Monberaut who had been recommended by General Gage as a man of substance and of influence among the French and Indians.[21] Gage had reason to believe that Mon-

[18] John Stuart (1718-79) after a varied mercantile and naval career, settled in Charlestown; was appointed Superintendent for Indian Affairs, which office he held until his death, remaining loyal to the Crown during the American Revolution. See Alden's *John Stuart.*

[19] Gage to Stuart, March 31, 1764, Gage Papers; Alden, *John Stuart,* pp. 193, 197-199.

[20] Report of Johnstone to the Board of Trade, May 30, 1764, *MPAED,* I, 150; Johnstone to Halifax, October 31, 1764, *ibid.,* I, 152.

[21] Gage to Stuart, March 31, 1764, Gage Papers.

beraut might be induced to cooperate with the new colonists, and if his services were won, the dangers confronting the British might be alleviated.

MONTAULT DE MONBERAUT

The Chevalier Montault de Monberaut* was a scion of that lesser French nobility which, throughout the seventeenth and eighteenth centuries, dispatched its heirs abroad to seek their fortunes in the western world. For them America held more promise than Versailles, and men like Frontenac, Bienville, and Monberaut all left their mark upon the wilderness. They blazed its trails, explored its river roads, and learned to call the red men sons and brothers as the English never could. Yet they never lost that pride of birth and caste which signified their aristocracy.

The Montauts were numerous—deucedly so, George Johnstone would declare—and traced their lineage back to close alliance with that Jeanne d'Albret who was the mother of the Bourbon line of kings. The Chevalier, the third son of Joseph-Hector de Montaut, Marquis de Monberaud, could also mention his connection with a Duc de Guienne, a Comte de Bigorre, and the Kings of Navarre and Aragon. Most recently his brother, Augustin-Francois, Comte de Montaut, had advanced the family honor by gaining a place in the household of the Dauphin's son, the Duc de Berry, who was destined to become the ill-fated Louis XVI of France.[22]

The younger Montaut was born May 7, 1718, at Palaminy, a village overlooking the Garonne River about a mile west of the town of Cazeres. The next day, at the parish church, the child was

* Neither the Chevalier himself nor his contemporaries ever achieved any orthographic consistency in using these names, and later historians have done no better. In accordance with the rather cavalier practices of eighteenth century spelling, the names appear as Montault, Montaut, Montberaud, Monberaut, and so on. It seemed most appropriate here, therefore, to adopt Monberaut's customary spelling, Montault de Monberaut, except where direct quotation requires a variant form.

22 Monberaut, "Mémoire Justificatif," p. 96, Gage Papers, hereafter cited as MJ. See also Jean Bernard Bossu, *Nouveaux Voyages aux Indes Occidentales*, 2nd ed. (Paris, 1768), II, 15n and Le Chenaye-Desbois et Badier, *Dictionnaire de la Noblesse* (Paris, 1869) IV, 89-90.

baptized Henri Elisabeth Aimé Montaut de Saint Sivier.[23] In all likelihood young Henri spent much of his youth in the hills of the Haute Garonne south of Toulouse, for he subsequently took the name of the village of Montberaud, located some four miles southeast of Cazeres, as his own distinctive appellation. By his own choice he would from then on be known as Montault de Monberaut.

Following the custom of his class and the calling of younger sons, Monberaut sought his fortune in the French army. On September 1, 1738, he was appointed lieutenant *reformé,* and at the age of twenty he began what proved to be a quarter of a century of service as an officer in the colony of Louisiana. Monberaut secured permanent rank as lieutenant on January 1, 1744, was commissioned captain *reformé* June 1, 1749, and on October 1, 1750, he was confirmed as captain *en pied.*[24] He had distinguished himself sufficiently by 1754, to be dispatched to Fort Toulouse as deputy commander under M. de Massé. The following year he succeeded to the post of commandant, and shortly thereafter he enrolled his elder son, Louis Augustin, Sieur de Montaut, as a cadet in the royal forces.[25]

At that strategic location in the heart of the Alabama country and in close proximity to the Creek Nation, Monberaut played an important role in French and Indian affairs as the struggle for control of North America reached its climax.

Fort Toulouse, the chief bastion defending French Louisiana against the incursions of Georgians and Carolinians and their Indian allies, was a typical frontier post. Built upon the banks of the Coosa River, not far from modern Wetumpka, Alabama, it had

[23] Dossier Montaut de Saint Sivier, Archives de France (Paris), Marine, C 7 215.

[24] MJ, p. 2 (pp. 72-73 of this translation. Future references will include only page numbers in parentheses); Monberaut to Gage, April 11, 1765, Gage Papers; Archives de France (Paris), Marine C 7 215.

[25] MJ, p. 8 (70); Alden, *John Stuart,* p. 54; Daniel H. Thomas, "Fort Toulouse," *Alabama Historical Quarterly,* XXII (1960), 185; Stuart to Gage, August 30, 1765: Colonial Office 5/72: 113-116 (photostatic copies in the Library of Congress, Washington, D. C.). Archives National (Paris), Colonies, D2C51: 189-196, and D2C51, Nos. 6, 8, 10, 13, 19, 35, 47 (transcripts in the Library of Congress).

been renovated when Monberaut arrived and boasted a palisade and ditch which gave it a formidable appearance. Its looks were deceiving, however, for the garrison numbered only forty to fifty men and officers, and its walls mounted but six guns.[26] The value of Fort Toulouse lay in its very existence as a point from whence the French might influence neighboring tribes, and in that, everything depended upon the abilities of its commandant.[27]

To his task Montault de Monberaut brought very considerable gifts, particularly a flair for languages, which won for him "une grande réputation" among the Indians of Alabama. "He is distinguished among these people," wrote the French traveler Bossu, "for the high-spirited harangues which he delivers in a manner quite akin to theirs." They hailed him as a "man of parts, that is to say a hero or a man *par excellence*."[28] The vicissitudes of his situation required all that and more, for Louis de Kerlérec, Governor of Louisiana, hoped to win the whole of the Creek Nation to the cause of France, and the commandant at Fort Toulouse was the chief agent of that policy. Unhappily, French colonial regulations made effective competition with the English traders difficult at best, and after 1756, the supply of goods from France stopped altogether. Not only were such posts as the one among the Alabamas devoid of gifts to hold the Indians' friendship, their garrisons were forced to trade with itinerant English merchants in order to supply their own basic needs.

Edmond Atkin, southern Indian Superintendent for the British, paid conscious tribute to men like Monberaut when he described the French commanders at the frontier posts as

> men of the greatest Knowledge and Experience, by early and long service . . . who rest their hopes of Preferment on their own Behaviour, and who on all Occasions support the Honour and Dignity of the French Nation, and watch all opportunities to turn

[26] Thomas, pp. 192-193, 203; Wilbur R. Jacobs, *Indians of the Southern Colonial Frontier, The Edmond Atkin Report and the Plan of 1755* (Columbia, S.C., 1954), 60.
[27] Alden, *John Stuart*, p. 53.
[28] Bossu, II, 15-16.

every Occurrence to their own Advantage, or to the Disadvantage of Great Britain and her colonies.[29]

In further analyzing his enemy's strength, Atkin noted a characteristic which Monberaut subsequently displayed in English service and certainly developed while in the French:

> It is no small addition to the influence of the French, that their Officers allways on the spot, both prevent Abuses being offer'd to the Indians by particular Persons, and also never fail to demand immediate Satisfaction for any Injuries or Insults offer'd by them; which is the more readily complied with. Whereas we not being in the like Condition to demand such Satisfaction for any offences, are obliged to put up with them, and are therefore slighted. . . .[30]

The English had little reason to congratulate themselves upon their southern Indian policy in the 1756-63 period. Promises of friendship were exchanged, but in spite of a virtual monopoly of trade goods and British possession of the *ultima ratio* of superior power, many Indian towns and chiefs remained pro-French. Notable among the latter was The Mortar, a confirmed Francophile and perhaps the most talented Creek chieftain of his generation. While Monberaut commanded at Fort Toulouse, The Mortar lived at Okfuskie, not more than thirty miles away. The two became so well acquainted that The Mortar later declared, according to Monberaut, that he had been nourished as a child upon the Frenchman's knees.[31] Certainly the bellicose Creek was far more amenable to the Chevalier's arguments than to the repeated pleas of the English whose messages he usually ignored—after he had lifted a sizeable number of their scalps.[32]

Personal influence among the savages is difficult to assess, but the failure of the English to win the Creeks to their side must be attributed to Monberaut's popularity and influence.[33] His most

[29] Jacobs, pp. 7-8, 12.

[30] *Ibid.*

[31] MJ, p. 151 (175-176).

[32] On The Mortar's activities prior to 1764 see Alden, *John Stuart, passim.*

[33] Jacobs, pp. 11-12. Monberaut's activities are also described in Captain Raymond Demere's letter of November 25, 1756, in Allen D. Candler (ed.), *The Colonial Records of the State of Georgia* (Atlanta, 1907), XVI, 147-148.

outstanding diplomatic success, however, was with the Cherokees. "I not only negotiated the peace which the French and the Alabamas made with the Cherokees," he boasted, "but I persuaded that Nation away from the English alliance and laid the first foundation of the sanguinary war that they made on them."[34] In contributing to the outbreak of the Cherokee War, Monberaut brought a touch of irony to history, for it was during that bloody conflict that John Stuart gained recognition for his skillful handling of the Indians—which recognition led to his appointment as Superintendent of Indian Affairs for the southern colonies. On the other hand, Stuart learned his lessons from the Cherokees as a prisoner ("I forged the first links of the chain which bound him," Monberaut declared) and was in fact most lucky that he was not dispatched by a French-inspired tomahawk, for he was a member of the unfortunate Fort Loudoun garrison massacred by the Indians in 1760. Among the victorious tribesmen was Monberaut's friend The Mortar.[35]

In addition to the ever-present task of maintaining French influence among the savages, Monberaut was plagued during his tenure at Fort Toulouse by recurrent disputes with the Jesuit missionaries stationed at the French outpost. Good Catholic though he was, the Chevalier became an avowed enemy of the Jesuits, probably because they sought to interfere with his methods of influencing the Indians. Reciprocating his animosity, the missionaries sought his removal. Père Maximillian Le Roi was the last of the meddlesome priests to annoy the commandant. A letter addressed to the governor, requesting Monberaut's recall, was entrusted by the Jesuit to a soldier of the garrison who promptly delivered it to his commanding officer. When next they met, Monberaut inquired of Père Le Roi if perchance he had written anything derogatory of the commandant to the officials of the province. The good father protested, by all that was holy, that he was innocent of any such action, upon which Monberaut vehemently berated and de-

[34] MJ, p. 8 (69-70).

[35] Stuart to Gage, January 3, 1765; Stuart to Pownall, January 24, 1765, Colonial Office 5/72: 99-101; MJ, p. 7 (69-70); and see Alden's account of the Cherokee War in *John Stuart*, chaps. VII-VIII, especially pp. 116-118.

nounced him as a knave and a liar. The incriminating letter was nailed to the gate of the fort, and while it remained there, no Jesuit troubled the Alabamas.[36]

The Church's version of this affair attributes Père Le Roi's hasty departure to his unpopular denunciation of the sale of liquor to the Indians, a practice which he decried as leading to drunkenness and every sort of crime.[37] According to John Stuart, *l'affaire* Le Roi was of secondary importance in bringing about Monberaut's subsequent removal from Fort Toulouse. Excessive expenditures, rather than immorality, he claimed, caused Governor Kerlérec to recall the Chevalier.[38] Stuart's charge of excess spending cannot be supported, however, and the official record is quite clear: Monberaut resigned his commission in 1762, on the honorable ground of poor health. Both the Chevalier and Governor Kerlérec felt justified in requesting a suitable decoration, the Croix de St. Louis, and a pension for the retired commandant of Fort Toulouse. Kerlérec's repeated urging of Monberaut's claim elicited the Duc de Choiseul's promise to see what might be done with regard to the pension, but, Choiseul advised, the Croix de St. Louis was out of the question as His Majesty Louis XV absolutely refused to grant that honor to any officer who resigned his commission.[39] Firmly convinced that he deserved the commendation, too proud and unbending to accept the rejection of his claim, Monberaut leaped to the unwarranted conclusion that the grant had, in fact, been made. His sensitivity on this point is evident in every reference to the Croix de St. Louis, and not until his return to France in 1769, did he admit to the disappointment of his hopes. Happily, his brother the Count was then able to ease his pain by procuring for him the long overdue pension.

Monberaut was relieved of the command of the Alabama fort by February 1759, and the Society of Jesus seems to have enjoyed the last word in their encounter; his successor was the brother of a

[36] Bossu, II, 15-16.

[37] John G. Shea, *History of the Catholic Church in the United States* (New York, 1886), I, 584-585.

[38] Stuart to Gage, August 30, 1765, Colonial Office 5/72: 113-116.

[39] Archives de France, Marine C 7 215; Colonies C 13 A, 43: 21, 101.

prominent Jesuit missionary.[40] That gentleman, M. Aubert, the Executive Officer of Fort Condé at Mobile, fell ill on the trip northward and did not reach Fort Toulouse until the end of April. Monberaut spent some time briefing Aubert (and also the itinerant M. Bossu, who had wanted the command) on local conditions, and in May he withdrew to his estate near Mobile.[41]

If the Chevalier's enemies were sufficiently influential to effect his removal from the Alabama post, his services were nonetheless valued at New Orleans. French officials did not hesitate to summon him to a council of war when his knowledge and advice were needed in negotiations with the Alabama Indians during the summer of 1760.[42]

Monberaut apparently devoted most of his attention to improving his private fortune, for in 1763 he petitioned the governor of Louisiana and was granted confirmation of ownership of a tract of land on the Fowl River, south-southwest of Mobile. There Monberaut developed a plantation known as Lisloy.[43] The estate's broad acres enabled the veteran and his two sons—the elder born about 1747, and the younger five years later—to support a comfortable existence by breeding cattle which were pastured in the low, swampy land between the rivers and the coast. Monberaut claimed that he possessed 500 cattle and 50 horses, not to mention flocks of sheep and pigs. His domestic household included a family of eight who had long followed his fortunes, and he owned 26 Negro slaves. Lisloy boasted a manor house, well-filled barns, a good garden, dairies, stables, parks, the whole enclosed by rail fences. Its master

[40] Bossu, II, 16.

[41] MJ, p. 8 (70n.); Bossu, II, 15, 63.

[42] Conseil de Guerre de la Mobile, June 24, 1760, Archives du Ministère des Colonies, Ser. C 13, Vol. original 42, Années 1760-61, Mississippi Provincial Archives. French Dominion, XXXI (transcripts).

[43] Monberaut's "Etat des Biens que j'avois sur le territoire cédé aux anglais en 1763," Colonial Office 5/71: 303; Translated Records, pp. 7-9, Office of the Secretary of State, Montgomery, Ala. Peter J. Hamilton, *Colonial Mobile*, rev. ed. (Mobile, 1952), 162-163. Hamilton located Lisloy between the headwaters of Bayou Labatterie and Fowl River. An English officer who visited Lisloy described it as situated 27 miles from Mobile on the coast on the way to New Orleans (Maclellan to Johnstone, November 15, 1764, Gage Papers). Monberaut merely declared that it was on the Fowl River, its adjacent lands lying between the Fowl and Labatterie Rivers and the coast.

maintained a boat manned by his slaves, thereby providing himself with easy access to and from Mobile. A second estate added to Monberaut's income through its farm produce. Located ten leagues north of Mobile on the Choctaw River, now the Tombigbee, it consisted of two farms facing one another across half a league of river frontage. Probably worked only part of the year, this place included a house, some Negro cabins, and a run-down mill. Monberaut also owned or shared property with a son-in-law a short distance from New Orleans where he had a planing mill, some slaves, and more cattle. Finally, Monberaut and his elder son, Louis Augustin, owned or held town houses in Mobile. The extent and value of his possessions, as well as his social status, clearly marked the Chevalier as a man of distinction on the Gulf Coast.[44]

The cession of Louisiana east of the Mississippi placed Monberaut in the awkward position of having to give up either his home, which he would probably be forced to sell at a loss, or his allegiance to France. News of the cession of the Isle of Orleans to Spain had not as yet reached Louisiana, but in any case, Monberaut was not eager to return to New Orleans, for he had quarreled with both Governor Kerlérec and M. d'Abbadie, commandant of the French forces.[45] If he could obtain a favorable situation at the hands of the English, it would be to his best interests to remain in British West Florida.

The Deputy Superintendent of Indian Affairs

Caught between an unfriendly administration in New Orleans and the new British masters of Mobile, Montault de Monberaut rested uneasily at Lisloy. Sentiment tied him to France—self-interest to West Florida. Happily, however, the uncertainties of Anglo-Indian relations opened an avenue for the exercise of the Frenchman's talents. Knowing and known to the red men, he saw

[44] Monberaut's "Etat des Biens," Colonial Office 5/71: 303; Monberaut to Johnstone and Stuart, December 13, 1764, MJ, p. 90.

[45] Monberaut to Aubry, March 7, 1765, MJ, p. 12; Alden, *John Stuart*, p. 210 n.

that he might safeguard his estate and secure his future by entering British service.

Lieutenant Colonel James Robertson, Quartermaster General of the British army in North America, had been sent by General Gage to West Florida to provide the commander-in-chief with an eye-witness report on the new territories, and to Robertson the Chevalier made his first approach. Burdened with troubles and complaints, and anxious to return to a more salubrious climate, Robertson commended Monberaut to Gage because of his apparent influence with the Creek Indians and his standing among the French inhabitants of West Florida. The general, greatly concerned with both the establishment and the cost of Indian policy, promptly advised the southern Indian Superintendent, Stuart, of his hopes for Monberaut:

> He has shown a desire, I suppose upon valuable consideration, to quit the French & become a British subject. If you find him an acquisition worth our acquiring, you may endeavor to prevail upon him to act with you in your Indian business. But I understand he is a gentleman of that temper that you must manage so with him as to lead him to act as you desire & direct, without his appearing to act under your orders. I shall write a civil letter to him, without mentioning anything particular to him, leaving it to you to settle matters as you shall judge most convenient after your acquaintance with him shall instruct you how far he may be useful.[46]

The "civil letter" to Monberaut expressed Gage's delight that one of the Chevalier's rank was inclined to remain at Mobile. Gage flattered the Frenchman on having two sons reputed to be "jeunes hommes de merite, et fort amiables," and assured Monberaut that a wise man whose mind was free and unprejudiced would find means of overcoming any obstacles to his and their advancement —a clear reference to Monberaut's Catholicism and the political disabilities that must follow under British law.[47] The ensuing correspondence clarified the issue posed by the Chevalier's loyalty to his faith, and on September 29, 1764, Gage advised Monberaut that in view of his religion it would be impossible to enlist him in

[46] Gage to Stuart, March 31, 1764, Gage Papers; Colonial Office 5/72: 97.
[47] Gage to Monberaut, March 31, 1764, Gage Papers.

any official capacity.[48] The general simultaneously recommended to the commanding officer at Mobile that Monberaut be given "all the service in your power, to facilitate his emigration in as agreeable and advantageous a manner for himself and family, as you possibly can."[49]

Faced with the apparent collapse of his hopes, Monberaut opened negotiations for the sale of his estate. A prospective purchaser was found in a Mr. Jones who was willing to pay £600 sterling for Lisloy in behalf of Admiral Sir William Burnaby.[50]

Meanwhile, the British civil officials appointed to West Florida began to arrive. Far from the elegance of New France which they expected to find, they encountered only poverty and sickness and hordes of savages crying loudly for presents.[51] John Stuart reached Pensacola early in October; since the governor had not yet appeared, he went on to Mobile. During his first brief and unpleasant sojourn there, the superintendent was unable to contact Monberaut, who was ill, but upon returning to Pensacola, Stuart met the newly-arrived and greatly agitated governor. Johnstone was concerned over the state of Indian affairs; Stuart was displeased by both the attitudes and actions of the military commanders at Mobile and Pensacola. Unaware that Gage had broken off with Monberaut, they decided to avail themselves of the services of the man the commander-in-chief had recommended to them.[52]

Prompt action was imperative. Monberaut was known to be selling his property and toying with the idea of joining the Spaniards whose acquisition of New Orleans, rumored since May, was formally announced in Louisiana in October. The English hoped to win the loyalty of the Mobile French, and Lieutenant Alexander Maclellan, who visited Lisloy in November, reported that Monberaut appeared eager to serve Johnstone and gave evidence of

[48] Gage to Monberaut, September 29, 1764, Gage Papers.

[49] Gage to Officer Commanding at Mobile, September 28, 1764, Gage Papers.

[50] MJ, p. 6 (69); Maclellan to Johnstone, November 15, 1764, Gage Papers.

[51] Farmar to Gage, and Mackinnen to Gage, September 24, 1764, Gage Papers.

[52] Stuart to Gage, October 12, November 19 and 30, 1764, Gage Papers.

being more friendly toward the British than the Spanish. Monberaut, however, refused to commit himself.[53]

Early in December, Johnstone and Stuart went to Mobile to survey the Indian situation in the western half of the colony. They promptly opened direct negotiations with Monberaut. At the outset the Frenchman displayed his correspondence with Gage which concluded with the general's regrets that Monberaut's Roman faith precluded employment under the British Crown. Undeterred, Johnstone and Stuart declared that the office of Deputy Superintendent of Indian Affairs was not established by law but was a creation of convenience to which the restrictions against Roman Catholics would not apply.

During these negotiations, according to Monberaut, Johnstone foiled the projected sale of Lisloy by persuading Jacob Blackwell, the Customs Collector, to withhold payment in behalf of Admiral Burnaby.[54] With the approaching expiration of the eighteen-month period allowed the French for the disposition of their goods, Monberaut had no alternative but to join the English or sell his property at a loss.

After lengthy discussions, Monberaut proposed that the governor and superintendent should submit their offer in writing and that he should reply in like manner. On December 8, 1764, Johnstone and Stuart addressed a joint letter to Monberaut stating that his "profound knowledge" of Indian diplomacy demanded that they ask his help in obtaining a treaty which would ensure a peaceful transition from French to English dominion. After his "combat of passion and honor" over Roman Catholicism and Gallic patriotism, they asked that he take the oath of loyalty for only so long as he might serve in an official capacity. He should receive a provisional commission as Deputy Superintendent of Indian Affairs for British West Florida effective until word might come from England regarding a more permanent arrangement. His first duties should be to persuade The Mortar to meet with the British at a congress in either Mobile or Pensacola and to induce the Creeks to work in the British interest. To aid him in these efforts, £100

[53] Maclellan to Johnstone, November 15 and 20, 1764, Gage Papers.
[54] MJ, pp. 6-7 (69).

sterling should be placed at his disposal for the purchase of gifts.

For himself they offered a salary of £210 sterling per annum, of which £100 should be paid immediately upon his acceptance of their proposition. As it would be imperative for the deputy to maintain quarters in Mobile, the English officials offered to provide a house or £50 a year for rental and also to provide reimbursement for any extraordinary expenses. Finally, all of Monberaut's land titles should be confirmed, his children should be recommended for preferment in the British service, and application should be made to the ministry for a larger pension than the governor was empowered to grant.[55]

Monberaut's lengthy reply was revealing. First, seeing nothing in the proposal inconsistent with his honor, he accepted the offer even though it was less than entirely satisfactory. The oath and provisional commission were agreeable to him, but he wanted the time limit for the sale of his property extended until he should make his final decision with regard to permanent residency, and he asked the same consideration for a family which had followed his fortunes for a number of years. He requested permission to correspond directly with General Gage, the Board of Trade, and the ministry, and asked to be relieved of taking orders from anyone of inferior rank. He served notice that he expected the right to give advice on any matter concerning the Indians and to question any directive unless time and urgency made that impossible.

His first specific complaint concerned the inadequacy of the amount designated for his use. As he claimed to speak no English, Monberaut asked for an interpreter and a secretary who should be supported at provincial expense. Whatever the English offered as rent was acceptable, but he had that day agreed to take a house from Major Farmar for 700 *piastres gourdes,* and he would have to make up the balance himself. The salary was unsatisfactory, but he was willing to accept it and await an increase from the British ministry. He also asked that in the event of a successful negotiation, his son, Louis Augustin, might have the traditionally lucrative privilege of bearing the good news to the English court.

[55] Johnstone and Stuart to Monberaut, December 8, 1764, MJ, pp. 16-18 (82-84).

Monberaut then called attention to certain matters which would at once prove his usefulness to the colony and support his request for greater pay and allowances. The French, he noted, had found it to their advantage to be very generous with the Indians. Food had always been provided at the king's expense, and the Indians expected some small presents when they left, as well as victuals for their journey home. Impressing upon Johnstone and Stuart the need for continuing such French customs, he argued that in the exposed situation of West Florida strict economy must not be allowed to interfere with the conduct of Indian affairs.

To provide his new employers with additional justification for the larger salary he sought, the Chevalier enumerated the losses and expenses he would incur by accepting employment under the British; he estimated that his actual expenses would be three or four times greater than heretofore.

Of additional concern to Monberaut was the fear that his motive, which he professed to be the furtherance of the general good of mankind, might be mistaken for avarice. Moreover, his service to France's erstwhile foe might tempt his enemies to deprive him of the Croix de St. Louis for which he had been nominated in 1759, not to mention his French pension and the inheritance of family lands. The offer of a Spanish colonelcy was also jeopardized, as was his property lying within the territory ceded to Spain. In the event that he should lose any of these things, he asked the protection of the British Crown and a guarantee of indemnification.[56]

The brief reply signed by Johnstone and Stuart two days later stated:

> We agree entirely to the terms. The two hundred pounds shall be paid immediately; if we succeed in the treaty, your son shall be sent to England; but that everything that depends on us may be fixed, we now mark one hundred pounds p. annum to be allowed you for the rent of your house.
>
> The charge of Clerk will come under that of extraordinaries.[57]

There was no apparent dissatisfaction with the terms, but Stuart

[56] Monberaut to Johnstone and Stuart, December 13, 1764, MJ, pp. 19-30 (84-91).

[57] Johnstone and Stuart to Monberaut, December 15, 1764, MJ, p. 30 (91).

wrote to General Gage on January 3, 1765, that while an understanding had been reached with Monberaut, his pretensions were at first very high, and he would not become a British subject until he had assurances of something permanent from the ministry.[58] Johnstone, on the other hand, seemed to have no reservations. He found Monberaut to be a sensible person possessed of as strong a mind as he had ever found among the French. Unfortunately Major Farmar, disregarding the Chevalier's potential value, had turned him out of his house—and even out of a bed in his daughter-in-law's house—in favor of a sick officer, so that Monberaut had no place to sleep but on the floor! Both justice and the king's service, the governor declared, would be advanced by his employment as an Indian agent.[59]

Monberaut's account of the proceedings, directed to General Gage, indicated satisfaction at having made the best bargain that he could. His actions bespoke his earnest intentions. The new deputy superintendent promptly purchased a house in Mobile from Captain James Campbell, and then set about to persuade The Mortar to meet with the governor and superintendent at the earliest convenient date.[60]

The Indian Congresses of 1765

Governor Johnstone and Superintendent Stuart were eager to establish the Indian relations of West Florida on a firm basis as quickly as possible. Two separate congresses were planned, the first with the Francophile Choctaws and the traditionally friendly Chickasaws, the second with the warlike Creeks. The Choctaws, however, were in no hurry to meet with the English. Offended at not having been consulted about the transfer of the province from

[58] Stuart to Gage, January 3, 1765, Gage Papers; Colonial Office 5/72:99.

[59] Johnstone to Gage, January 2, 1765, Gage Papers.

[60] Monberaut to Gage, December 31, 1764, Gage Papers. At the same time, December 19, 1764, Monberaut petitioned for a grant of 100 acres "on the opposite side of the way." Both petitions were approved by the Council on January 7, 1765. He was also granted Pensacola town lot No. 130 on February 7, 1765. See Howard, *British West Florida*, pp. 50, 57.

French to British rule, they sulked and refused to interrupt or curtail their hunting season merely to discuss a treaty with the English. It was March 1765 before the first of the Indian congresses met in Mobile.

Deputy Superintendent Monberaut having retired to Lisloy to make arrangements for an indefinite stay at Mobile, the preparations for receiving the Chickasaws and Choctaws were left to the British. Stuart contracted with Jacob Blackwell, the customs collector at Mobile, to supply meat for the Mobile congress, and in turn Blackwell subcontracted with Christopher Miller, a nephew of Major Farmar, but it soon became apparent that the entrepreneurs would be unable to meet the superintendent's needs. Faced with the imminent arrival of the two Indian tribes in late February, Stuart hurried to Lisloy on the pretext of paying a friendly visit and there laid his problem before Monberaut, whom he asked to supply the necessary animals. Monberaut agreed and also promised to provide calves for the superintendent's table so that he might serve those delicacies suitable to his position. With his mind put at ease by the Frenchman's assurances, Stuart settled down to enjoy a few days of his lieutenant's noted hospitality.[61]

Returning to Mobile in his host's boat, Stuart found that Tomatle Mingo, chief of the Conchatys, and forty of his braves had already reached the town. Nor was that all, for newly-arrived traders informed him that on the way they had passed many more savages who would be there in a few days. By means of the returning boat, Stuart sent word to Lisloy that Blackwell had promised to meet the emergency with thirty head of cattle, but for the rest he was relying on the Chevalier.[62]

Two days later, on February 27, Stuart sent his secretary, John McGillivray, to Monberaut with the alarming news that Blackwell had reneged. The superintendent begged his deputy to send whatever beef he could, and Monberaut assured McGillivray that although he could not guarantee the quality of the animals, he would send the best that he could find.[63]

61 MJ, pp. 57-58 (108-109).
62 Stuart to Monberaut, February 25, 1765, MJ, pp. 58-59 (109-110).
63 Stuart to Monberaut, February 27, 1765, MJ, pp. 59-60 (110).

As the Indians began to assemble in Mobile, Monberaut moved into the town house which he had purchased from Captain Campbell and invited Stuart to share his quarters. The arrangement was clearly advantageous to the superintendent, for he was able to take diplomatic advantage of the good impressions made by Monberaut's hospitality, and at the same time he was relieved of the responsibility of providing the entertainment. Frequently Monberaut had to set a table for a dozen great-medal-chiefs and as many notables of the town, and Stuart was not prepared for such festivities, much as he might have enjoyed them.[64] Domiciled together, the superintendent and his deputy could most easily concert their actions during the congress, and Monberaut would always be on hand to advise Stuart concerning the French customs which the English had promised to continue.

By mid-March, representatives of the Chickasaw Nation and the Western Division and Six Villages of the Choctaws had assembled in Mobile. Monberaut declared that he had never seen so many Indians. "I think that the villages were abandoned while the savages hurried to attend the first parley with the English!" Representatives of the Eastern Division of the Choctaws were delayed by a smallpox epidemic, and seeing that further postponement would entail exorbitant expenditures, Stuart proceeded to open negotiations on March 26 with the Great or Western Division and with the Six Villages, whose spokesmen were the most numerous present.[65] Alabama Mingo, Nashuba Mingo, Tomatle Mingo, and the Chickasaw chief Payamataha were the principal Indian negotiators; Johnstone, Stuart, Monberaut, and the recently arrived

[64] On the social life of the Mobile congress and Stuart's tippling, see MJ, pp. 86-87 (130); and David Wedderburn to Alexander Wedderburn, April 14, 1765, Wedderburn Papers, William L. Clements Library, Ann Arbor, Michigan, in which the officer states that "for some weeks past I have dined with forty or fifty Indians in the room."

[65] Alden, *John Stuart,* p. 201, states that representatives of the Six Villages were not present at the first conference. Monberaut's statement appears to be accurate since only one chief of the Eastern Division took part in the deliberations, while several representatives of the Six Villages participated. See letter from Monberaut to Gage, March 19, and April 11, 1765, Gage Papers; and *MPAED,* I, 26-38, 215-253.

Lieutenant Colonel David Wedderburn of the 22nd Regiment,[66] headed the British party.

After the customary preliminaries, Johnstone addressed the Indians and presented Stuart as "the General Protector of all your Rights." He then introduced Deputy Superintendent Montault de Monberaut, saying:

> . . . as it has been the misfortune of many among you to pursue different interests from us in the former part of your life, which often leaves a Jealousy in the mind on a Subsequent Reconcilement, in order to Remove every Circumstance of this kind which might Interrupt the perfect pleasure [of] a Sincere Peace . . . we have therefore made Choice of Monsieur Montbereaut, who was your ancient Friend to manage the affairs of the Indians in this Province under us. . . .[67]

Johnstone then outlined the objectives of the congress: peace among the Choctaws, Chickasaws, and English; curtailment of the sale of liquor in the Indian Nations; establishment of armorers and commissaries at Fort Tombecbe; regulation of trade prices, and settlement of a definite boundary between the province and the Indians' territory which would allow the English sufficient land for their agricultural needs.

The ten days of the congress were taken up with speeches, private discussions, and ceremonial dances. On the second day, Monberaut delivered an oration which had been edited (but scarcely changed) by the governor. Pointing out to the Indians that the French had departed, never to return, and that the English alone could supply their needs, the deputy superintendent besought his children, the red men, to follow both his advice and his example and cooperate with their new masters. He sharpened his appeal by claiming that only his great concern for the Indians had prevented his departure for France and had led him to accept employment with the British. Such a sacrifice, he pleaded, should

[66] On David Wedderburn see Robert R. Rea, "Outpost of Empire: David Wedderburn at Mobile," *Alabama Review*, VII (1954), 217-232.

[67] *MPAED*, I, 216-217; similar sentiments were expressed by Stuart, *ibid.*, p. 231.

serve as ample evidence of his concern and of the satisfaction they might expect from Stuart and Johnstone.[68]

In their official report of the Congress of Mobile, Johnstone and Stuart indicated that no great difficulty was encountered in securing agreement with the savages, but Monberaut declared, without relating the circumstances, that Tomatle Mingo threatened to leave without waiting for the English to distribute their presents.[69] At any rate, by April 2 all difficulties were settled, and the savages displayed their good will by conferring Indian names and titles upon the colonial officials. Johnstone became Mongoulachimataha; Stuart, Choctawmataha Chito; Wedderburn was designated Fannimingomataha; and Monberaut, Inhoulactimataha.

It is ironic to note that the very act which signified harmony between the British and the Indians nearly caused a rift among the colonial officials. According to Monberaut, Chulustamastabe, a stalwart Anglophile who conducted the name-giving ceremony, wished to dub the Chevalier Inhoulactimataha. Johnstone objected on the ground that it was too similar to his own title. Immediately discerning the governor's jealous nature, the feeble but crafty Alabama Mingo moved to exploit the situation to his people's benefit and proposed for Monberaut the more impressive title of Choctawoulactymataha. Happily, the interpreter, Favre, silenced the cunning chieftain before the governor could take umbrage at the suggestion.[70]

Dissension was prevented for the time, and on April 4, the final ceremonies were held and the treaty signed which granted to the English all that they had initially asked.[71] The Indians returned to their homes, Governor Johnstone returned to Pensacola, and Stuart and his deputy settled down to await the arrival of the remaining Choctaw representatives.

[68] MJ, pp. 111-113 (147-149); "Copie De La harrangue que M. Le Chevalier De Montault De Monberaut . . . a fait aux Nations Tchikachas et Tchaktas . . . Le 27e Mars 1765," Gage Papers. Johnstone's Report in *MPAED,* I, 236, only mentions that Monberaut spoke.

[69] MJ, pp. 103-104 (141-142); *MPAED,* I, 215-255.

[70] MJ, pp. 104-105 (142); *MPAED,* I, 243. Chulustamastabe seems to have been particularly fond of Monberaut, *MPAED,* I, 225.

[71] *MPAED,* I, 249-254.

The chiefs and warriors of the Eastern Division presented themselves in Mobile on April 22.[72] To Stuart's surprise, however, they were in a surly mood and far more ill-disposed toward the British than the Great Division had been. The superintendent's request that they surrender their French medals and commissions in order to receive those of the English, as the rest of the Choctaws had done, was met with a prompt refusal. In a pointed simile their spokesman compared the English to "snakes who hide in the grass, lying in wait for travelers, and strike them on the leg," for like the serpent, the English gave no warning until the pain began.[73] Without deigning to hear Stuart's reply, the Indians retired to deliberate among themselves. Eventually they sent word to the superintendent that they had determined not to give up their French decorations.

With more ardor than tact, Stuart swore that the savages should be forcibly deprived of their French trinkets and English commissions given to new chieftains who would be beholden to the English. Sensing the disastrous effect that such a threat would have on the negotiations, Monberaut asked permission to speak to the recalcitrant red men. This Stuart granted and, leaving the business in his deputy's hands, he retired with Colonel Wedderburn to spend two days at Francis Morcier's plantation.[74]

During the two days the Chevalier enjoyed full responsibility for the negotiations, the Indians were dissuaded from their hostile attitude. First, Monberaut, accompanied by Arthur Gordon, secretary for the congress,[75] went to the Choctaws and explained the fate awaiting any chief who refused to accept the English commissions. His touching description of the sadness he would feel at seeing the high brought low and others raised up in their places

[72] Monberaut to Gage, April 11, 1765, Gage Papers; Alden, *John Stuart*, p. 201.

[73] MJ, p. 114 (150).

[74] Francis Morcier (Moresier, Morzier, Mozier) was a French protestant who settled near Mobile and was appointed to the provincial Council by Governor Johnstone.

[75] Arthur Gordon was a lawyer, justice of the peace, member of the Council, and secretary to the Mobile congress. Monberaut requested his company because he spoke French.

had a telling effect upon the jealous savages. He then took up the Indians' reptilian simile—now further elaborated upon by a comparison of the British to crayfish which seemed to await a victim with hospitably open arms when in reality they only waited to seize him in their claws. The task which had stymied Stuart posed no great problem for the Frenchman with his flair for Indian rhetoric; he adroitly turned off their analogies with contempt and showed that he considered them mere insolences.

When Stuart returned, he found that his deputy had been successfully employed, and on April 27, the superintendent presided at the final meeting with the Choctaws of the Eastern Division. They surrendered their French medals, but in so doing, they thrice saluted Monberaut before turning them over to Stuart. Speeches followed in which they accorded Monberaut, whom they referred to as their "father," much of the credit for an amicable settlement. After signing a most satisfactory treaty, the Choctaws departed—not without grumbling about the inferior trade goods which Stuart had foisted on them.[76]

Upon the successful issue of the congresses at Mobile, Monberaut presented two bills for his extraordinary expenses. In one he asked reimbursement of 172 *piastres* and 5 *escalins* for "daily expenses," and in the second he listed candles, wine, and other articles totaling 182 *piastres.* Stuart examined the accounts and recommended that he combine them and present a single bill.

While Monberaut was trying to get his accounts settled, he received a letter from his son Louis Augustin bearing the good news that The Mortar had agreed to meet with the English in Pensacola. He hurried to inform the superintendent, whom he found in earnest and agitated conversation with McGillivray. The two Scots were unaware that Monberaut knew enough English to follow their discussion—nor did the Chevalier disabuse them. Instead, he listened with great interest while Stuart jealously deplored the fact that Monberaut's credit among the Choctaws had been raised so much higher as a result of the recent negotiations. After hearing McGillivray calm his superior with assurances that what seemed

[76] MJ, pp. 115-119 (150-154); Alden, *John Stuart,* pp. 201-202.

a threat to Stuart could doubtless be used to accomplish the deputy's ruin, Monberaut remained only long enough to ascertain that Stuart had also received word of The Mortar's change of heart.

Shortly thereafter, McGillivray called for Monberaut's accounts, explaining that Stuart wished to have everything pertaining to the Mobile Congress settled before his departure for Pensacola. Monberaut curtly informed Stuart's secretary that he had presented his accounts, revised them according to the superintendent's recommendations, and resubmitted them. As he neither wished to change them further nor to allow anyone else to tamper with them, he had no more to say on the subject. McGillivray answered with an impertinence which Monberaut would have punished at once had he not realized that in so doing he would fall into his adversaries' trap. He therefore contented himself with reporting the secretary's insolence to Stuart in the vain hope of obtaining satisfaction.

Disappointed in that, he resorted to a letter of protest setting forth McGillivray's improper behavior and including another detailed account of his expenses, which he reckoned by then to have reached 2200 *piastres*, taking into consideration all the costs from the beginning of his appointment as deputy superintendent. Previously he had ignored the "indecencies" of Stuart's suite, attributing them to ignorance, but he was now convinced that they were committed out of malice and ought to be brought into the open. He concluded with a request that all further dealing between himself and Stuart be conducted without the mediation of the latter's secretary. Stuart declined to answer in writing but sent Charles Stuart to inform Monberaut that their differences would be settled in Pensacola.[77] Thereby, the Chevalier, who might otherwise have declined to serve, was induced to join in the negotiations with the Creeks.

The news which had reached Monberaut at Mobile represented a major diplomatic breakthrough in West Florida Indian relations. Until that time the Upper Creek chieftain, The Mortar, had resolutely refused to have anything to do with the British on the Gulf,

[77] MJ, pp. 87-91 (130-133).

preferring rather to deal with the South Carolinians and Georgians. The Mortar's intractability had been of primary concern to Johnstone and Stuart who realized that there would be little peace or opportunity for the infant colony to develop unless the Creeks agreed to a treaty ceding land around the provincial capital and regulating the conditions of trade.

In the summer of 1764, The Mortar had sent Stuart a "talk" in which he stated that he would have no intercourse with West Florida. The Creeks, he said, had long traded with the towns on the Atlantic, and having been born after the paths had been made, he had no inclination to change them.[78] Again in November 1764, Johnstone and Stuart besought the Upper Creeks to discuss a treaty, but again they failed. Jealous of their business, the seaboard merchants made every effort to maintain their monopoly of the Indian trade, and their intrigues were successful until, at the behest of the colonial government, Monberaut sent his son as a pledge of the good faith of the British in West Florida.[79]

Because The Mortar was the key figure in, and principal obstacle to the negotiations, Johnstone and Stuart had expressly requested Monberaut to contact him and entice him to the colony. Monberaut readily undertook the task, his first step being to ascertain the winter hunting grounds each of the Creek chiefs had chosen. Topalga, a minor Creek chief who was an intimate of The Mortar and had previously aided Monberaut, chanced to be hunting in the area between Mobile and Pensacola. Monberaut persuaded him, for a price, to abandon his sport and guide Louis Augustin de Montaut to the great chief. To his son, the deputy superintendent entrusted his letter to The Mortar, along with instructions that it was to be read to the chieftain in the presence of the leading men of the Creek Nation in order that all might know that Monberaut stood with the English and supported their proposals.[80]

78 "Talk" sent from The Mortar to Stuart, July 22, 1764, West Florida Transcripts, State Department of Archives and History, Montgomery, Alabama.

79 Alden, *John Stuart*, pp. 204-205.

80 Monberaut to Yahatasky Stonaké, February 3, 1765, Gage Papers (a copy was also appended to the MJ); "Copie du Memoire Instructif pour le Sieur de Montaut," Gage Papers.

While the Chevalier was preparing for the Mobile congress, the Sieur de Montaut was having his own difficulties. From Little Talisi, about seven miles northeast of Fort Toulouse, Louis Augustin wrote to his father of frustrating delays and hardships which had beset his party. As it was necessary for the Indians to provide food for the entourage, they had often remained encamped four or five days while the red men hunted. Heavy rains retarded their progress, and when Topalga's wife was injured by a fall from her horse, the whole train had to bivouac at Fort Toulouse. Realizing that further delays would ensue, Montaut sent one of Topalga's braves to The Mortar's village with a gift of tobacco and sticks with which the chief might indicate the date on which he would meet the British emissary in order to hear Monberaut's "talk." Three weeks passed before the messenger returned with the frustrating news that while most of the Creeks were agreeable to meeting the English, The Mortar had joined the Cherokees to continue his hunting and could not be located. In despair Montaut sought new instructions from his father.[81]

Monberaut sent his son a cheerful letter relating the success of the Mobile congress and suggesting that the establishment of friendly relations between the Choctaws and the British might influence The Mortar to come to Pensacola. He pointed out that Stuart would soon be leaving West Florida for Charlestown and stressed the urgency of Montaut's mission. His strongest argument, however, was the long-standing friendship that existed between the Creeks and the sometime French commandant in their lands, and he did not hesitate to term The Mortar "ingrate" if he failed to heed his message.[82]

Montaut left no record of his delivery of the Chevalier's letter or the circumstances attending the Creek decision to treat with the British in West Florida, but news of his ultimate success hastened Stuart's departure for Pensacola. On May 24, word came that The Mortar was encamped near the town, but fearing reprisals for the murder of a white man by two Tallapoosas, the Creeks would not come into Pensacola. Monberaut volunteered to go out to the In-

[81] Montaut to Monberaut, March 18, 1765, Gage Papers.
[82] Monberaut to Montaut, March 29, 1765, Gage Papers.

dian camp and try to persuade them to enter the town. He asked Colonel Wedderburn, who spoke French fluently, to accompany him, for he was wary of the superintendent's jealousy and anxious to have an incontrovertible witness. In addition to Wedderburn, two interpreters, Renochon and Forestal, Lt. Alexander Maclellan (later provincial Deputy Secretary), and several soldiers made up the party that escorted Monberaut.

When the little band reached the crest of a hill overlooking the valley in which the Indians had established their camp, they were met by a delegation of The Mortar's principal chiefs and warriors who carried word that their great chief would be pleased to receive his "father" whom he had believed dead. After the Chevalier introduced Wedderburn as a "great warrior, commander of troops, and my special friend," Monberaut and the young Scottish officer were escorted into the camp while the savages chanted peacefully. The Mortar received them under an arbor of green boughs, and all the red men listened attentively while Monberaut first reproached them for their misdeeds and then outlined the course they should follow in presenting themselves to the governor and the superintendent.[83] After consultation among themselves, the Indians decided to be governed by their "father's" advice.

Tremendously impressed by the Frenchman's influence over The Mortar, Wedderburn asked Monberaut to arrange an adoption between himself and the noble chieftain, and The Mortar declared that he would accept any friend of his "father" as his brother. After the adoption ceremony, all consulted together, working out in detail the procedure which the Indians should follow the next day. It was agreed that the British emissaries would meet the Indians at a creek bordering the town and lead them into the fort.

The Mortar's tribesmen accordingly moved in toward Pensacola, but just before they reached the creek, they halted and demanded that Stuart and Johnstone themselves should act as their escorts. Chagrined and understandably irritated, Monberaut dispatched interpreters to reproach them for their inconstancy, but to no avail.

[83] See the "Copie de la harrangue fait par M. le Chevalier de Montault de Monberaut . . . la veille de l'entreé des dittes Nations à Pansacolla," Gage Papers.

As a final resort the deputy superintendent sent his son to rebuke The Mortar for breaking his word. Reassured by the sight of Louis Augustin and persuaded by Monberaut's arguments, The Mortar offered no further obstruction and, meeting the Chevalier at the prearranged spot, he marched into Pensacola accompanied by the rest of the Creeks singing and dancing as they advanced.

After the Indians had crowded into the meeting place, the conference opened as planned. Monberaut interceded in their behalf, asking the English to withhold taking vengeance upon the whole tribe because of the irresponsible acts of a few young men. Johnstone and Stuart accepted the proffered white eagle-tails in token of their assent, and the Indians cheered lustily as the governor pronounced his disposition to pardon them. In replying to the governor, the Creeks rendered due credit to the Chevalier for his part in drawing them from their homes to Pensacola and for their actual meeting with the British. The first hurdle cleared, The Mortar was content to end the day's business and enjoy English hospitality.

The second day of the congress, May 27, was filled with speeches, and Monberaut heard Governor Johnstone declare, "We have . . . made Choice of Mr. Montbereau to manage the affairs of the Indians under us to remove all Jealousies, from those who formerly espoused another Interest." Superintendent Stuart further advised the Creeks that ". . . as the King's Business Calls me away from this Province, Monsieur de Montbereau will take Charge of your affairs in my absence. . . . You are so well acquainted with him, that my saying any thing further will be Needless."[84]

Illness kept the Chevalier from active participation on May 28 and forced him to remain in his quarters. John Stuart, however, accomplished what no Frenchman had ever been able to achieve. The Mortar had consistently refused to accept a French medal, but at his first private conference with the superintendent, he found Stuart seated on a heap of French medals which the Choctaws had exchanged for English gorgets. By explaining that the British medal was a sign of prestige, honor, and responsibility, Stuart

[84] *MPAED*, I, 192, 197.

whetted the proud chieftain's desire, and his feigned reluctance to bestow one upon The Mortar made it even keener. Finally the prized trinket was handed over, and for a while all went well; the treaty began to take shape.[85]

The English wanted to obtain an agreement similar to that which the Choctaws and Chickasaws had signed two months earlier. The Creeks, however, raised objections, and at first The Mortar refused even to discuss the all-important boundary question, insisting that as all of his Nation was not represented, any agreement would be invalid. In reality he feared that the English would demand confirmation of the cession made by Wolf King in 1764, which he erroneously believed to be larger than it was.

Hearing of the stalemate, Monberaut asked Colonel Wedderburn to arrange for The Mortar and ten of his principal warriors to come to his room, and through an interpreter the deputy endeavored to persuade the Creeks to accept the line to which the Choctaws had agreed. On this point Monberaut encountered more difficulty than in all the negotiations related to the Pensacola congress.

The Indians immediately asked, "Is it possible . . . that you, who at the time you were with the French so often exhorted us not to yield a bit of land to the English, you chide us today, and press us with so much fluency to give it up to them?"[86]

Monberaut was prepared for such an obvious question. He explained diplomatically that he had always had the best interests of "his children" at heart. When he had asked them to keep the English out of their lands, he had done so to save them from the horrors of civil war which would have resulted from some of the Creeks espousing the French cause while others acted in the British interest. Now that King George ruled all the lands east of the Mississippi, wherever they went the Indians would find only the English. It was, therefore, incumbent upon him, since he always acted for their welfare, to show them how to live in peace with their new masters.

Having allayed the Indians' anxiety on that point, Monberaut

[85] Alden, *John Stuart,* p. 206.
[86] MJ, p. 145 (171).

explained the exact boundaries of the area to be ceded and emphasized its smallness. He argued that to refuse the English the lands they asked would be to deny themselves subsistence when next they came to Pensacola for the annual gifts upon which the French had taught them to depend.[87]

The impact of Monberaut's words was recorded in The Mortar's speech on May 28. "As to the proposed boundary line," he declared, "I acknowledge I did not clearly understand its situation but am informed by Monsieur Monberaut that it runs along by the Forks of the Alibamont and Tombeckbé Rivers. . . ."[88]

Monberaut's indisposition prevented his further participation in the congress until the completion of the talks. For reasons undisclosed, Johnstone and Stuart agreed to hold the concluding formalities in the woods rather than in the town to which The Mortar had been so laboriously coaxed and where all the negotiations had been conducted. Monberaut felt certain that the Creeks had come to Pensacola "full of roguish tricks," and that he had been instrumental in thwarting the Indians' designs against British prestige, but in his absence Stuart and Johnstone fell into a trap. The Indians lured them out of the town and succeeded in signing the treaty where they had first wanted to hold the congress. Monberaut believed that had the governor intended to conclude the treaty in the woods, it would have been better to have conceded to the Creeks' first demand, for having once outwitted the British, the Indians were encouraged to further boldness.

The treaty had been worked out in every detail; only the signatures were lacking, but when the British arrived for the final ceremony, The Mortar had one more favor to ask for his people. First, however, he proposed that they return to town and have dinner. Johnstone and Stuart were at a loss to know what to do other than comply and await the eventual disclosure of The Mortar's request. He was not long in revealing that he sought an equalization of trade prices. Having recently returned from the Cherokee Nation, the Creek chief knew the prices they enjoyed and saw that the Creeks were suffering from discrimination. Johnstone and

[87] MJ, pp. 145-146 (171-172).
[88] *MPAED*, I, 202.

Stuart tried to convince him that price regulation was beyond their control, but to no avail. To their consternation, The Mortar replied that if that were the case, they could tear up the treaty for the Creeks were going home!

Monberaut had taken no part in the congress since his private meeting with The Mortar and had only second-hand knowledge of the unfortunate events which transpired in the woods. The following day, however, the British officials came to him and asked his help. In spite of his illness, he dressed and went to the meeting place where he found Johnstone haranguing the Indians, desperately trying to convince them that he lacked the authority to satisfy their demand.

As soon as the governor saw the Chevalier approaching, he said, "You have confidence in M. de Monberaut, ask him if it is in my power to grant you your demand." While the governor pleaded, Monberaut quickly outlined to Stuart his thoughts on the subject. The superintendent then asked Johnstone to abridge his oration so that Monberaut might speak.

The Frenchman went straight to the hearts of his audience by appealing to their long association in friendship and in war.

> You have testified to putting your confidence in me; you are right; I have never failed you; I will not fail you today. Give me evidence of your friendship by rendering yourselves amenable to the exhortation that I make you. Let the treaty remain, and have confidence in the good will that your fathers, the English, show you.[89]

The Mortar rose to reply:

> I have been invited from several places to go to hear "talks." I did not wish to go anywhere. My father over there finally sent a written "talk" which was carried to me by his son. He invited me to go hear yet other words which he and the English chiefs had to say to me. I have been raised as a child cherished on my father's knees, to whom I have never lied, and he will judge, himself, that the words which I am going to give him are not lies. I did not come here to grieve my father. Thus, I believe, since he tells me, that it is not in the English chief's power to grant me my

[89] MJ, pp. 145-146 (174-175).

> demands. There (showing the portrait of the King) is the father of all the red men and white men. These chiefs assure me that they are going to write to him, to the end that they will give us merchandise at a better price. I believe that since my father assures me of it. I am going to exhort my warriors to have patience until they have received the reply of the great chief of all the English.
>
> I also ask my father, M. de Monberaut, to say to the English chief that he ought not be aroused against me because I uphold the interests of my people. He says that he is the father of his; I am of mine![90]

Thus through the influence of Montault de Monberaut the last obstacle to a harmonious settlement was removed, and on June 4, the Treaty of Pensacola was signed. Within six months of Monberaut's appointment as deputy superintendent, Indian affairs in West Florida had been transformed from a state of imminent peril to one of promising, if precarious, peace.

The End of an Entente Cordiale

With the signing of the treaty, life in the capital of British West Florida began to assume a more normal aspect. Troops from Mobile returned to their station; the Creeks drifted back to their villages; and the colonial officials turned their attention to other matters. Monberaut remained at Pensacola until the second week of June, leaving for Mobile a few days before John Stuart set sail for Charlestown.[91] Prior to their parting, which was amicable enough, Stuart instructed his deputy "by all possible means to avoid Incurring any great Expense, But where you may Judge it absolutely necessary you will apply to His Excellency the Governor . . . for his directions and approbation." If circumstances prevented communication with Johnstone, Monberaut was ordered to seek

[90] MJ, pp. 150-152 (175-176).

[91] The congress ended June 4, the earliest date The Mortar could have departed; Monberaut states that he left eight days after The Mortar; Stuart sailed on June 15, and Monberaut had gone prior to that date, so he must have sailed for Mobile June 12-13. MJ, p. 127 (159); receipt date at Pensacola, June 10, 1765, Colonial Office 5/72: 110; Alden, *John Stuart*, p. 211.

the advice of the commanding officer at Mobile.[92] Accordingly, on June 19, the deputy superintendent addressed a report to Johnstone requesting the governor's advice on several matters.[93]

The local Indian chieftains had long enjoyed the privilege of taking their board with the French Indian agent when they were in Mobile. Since he had been given no specific instructions to continue this costly practice and his basic allocation was insufficient to cover the expense, Monberaut inquired if he might expect reimbursement for it in the future. If not, he proposed to discontinue it—a decision which would save money but might result in a loss of influence among the Indians.

The Chevalier further reported that upon reaching Mobile he had been welcomed by a pair of prominent and thirsty Choctaws. Two barrels of watered rum had been required for their immediate satisfaction. The deputy superintendent had consulted with Colonel Wedderburn who had approved the expenditure, but Giroud, the acting storekeeper, had refused to honor Monberaut's requisition until Wedderburn had assured him that he ran no financial risk. The sensitive Frenchman was persuaded that Giroud's inaction was a sign that he doubted the permanence of the Chevalier's employment.

Interpreters provided an additional source of annoyance. Favre, who had been ordered to Fort Tombecbe, refused to go because his health was poor and his private affairs would suffer in his absence. He chose to resign and asked for his salary and subsistence through June 18. Monberaut consequently released him and forwarded the request for his emoluments. Renochon, who had served as an interpreter at Pensacola, reported that during his absence

[92] Monberaut to Johnstone, June 19, 1765, Gage Papers; Stuart's instructions in Colonial Office 5/72: 103-104.

[93] Johnstone mentions "M. Monbereau having wrote me thirteen letters in the space of a week after his arrival" in Mobile, but no evidence of this correspondence has been found. Monberaut's letter of June 19 must have been the first of any such series, and the internal evidence as well as the date of Johnstone's reply (June 26) casts grave doubts upon the governor's veracity. Monberaut does not mention other correspondence, and he usually cites all possible evidence. No one but Johnstone ever saw the "thirteen letters"; had they existed it seems most likely he would have forwarded them to Stuart as he claimed they were "full of invective" against him.

Indians had raided his property, burned his buildings, and eaten about thirty pigs and cows. The redskins had allegedly carried off ten horses, and it was not certain whether those that remained belonged to Renochon or to someone else. Naturally Monberaut transmitted Renochon's request that he be compensated for losses incurred while engaged in his official duties.[94]

A few hours after the Chevalier dispatched this letter to Johnstone, Louis Augustin appeared with disturbing news. Returning by land from Pensacola, he had called on the interpreter Louis Forneret from whom he heard the rumor, attributed to John McGillivray, that Monberaut was about to be turned out of the British service. While the deputy was aware of the insecurity of his position, he had no idea that his affairs had reached a crisis. He felt he had most to fear from Stuart's jealousy, but since Stuart had given him detailed written instructions when he left for Mobile, Monberaut had presumed that he would not be disturbed before the British ministry's decision regarding his future employment reached West Florida.

The Chevalier was not a man to accept insult or dismissal without protest. In a memorial which he immediately addressed to the governor and the superintendent, he listed seventeen articles explaining the cause of his agitation and demanding that McGillivray's malice be punished. He then outlined the history of his employment and requested verification of his status in the provincial hierarchy, reminding his superiors, in the event that the report was not merely the product of envy, of the stipulations of their final agreement.

Although his epistle was conceived in the heat of passion, Monberaut was sufficiently realistic to appreciate the effect of his recent labors:

> At the time when you sought me out, gentlemen, the forces of His Britannic Majesty had not had the same success which they have had since. All the Nations who made war on the English are now subjugated and have been constrained to implore the clemency of the conqueror. . . . Circumstances being changed, my

[94] Monberaut to Johnstone, June 19, 1765, Gage Papers.

services are perhaps not as necessary as they appeared to be at the time when you sought me out.[95]

Monberaut clearly recognized that in view of his French nationality and Catholic faith, his employment was at best provisional, but he felt that his superiors owed him fair warning of dismissal and full accomplishment of the terms of their agreement. His letter contained the further advice that because his property in Louisiana was in danger of confiscation to the benefit of the king of either France or Spain, he proposed to send Louis Augustin to New Orleans. Should his own presence prove necessary, he demanded permission to leave the colony on that business. Although he hoped that any decision concerning his status might await word from England, he requested "a reply on which I can form a plan of action."[96]

George Johnstone was in no mood to receive an ultimatum or to pamper the tender pride of a Frenchman. Embroiled in violent arguments over protocol with the military authorities, he also found himself the center of that Anglo-Scottish vendetta which rent British politics from Westminster to West Florida. And in addition to these involvements, while the Indians had disappeared, disease had not. The colony was being decimated by a fever which hardened veterans swore was worse than any they had encountered in the islands and which took them off at a terrifying rate. His nerves raw, his patience exhausted, Johnstone claimed to be perplexed by Monberaut's memorial, but he was certain that the deputy must either possess "entire confidence" or be prevented from making trouble by "an entire separation." In this affair, at least, he could be the master of events. Keeping his own counsel, he "revolved those matters maturely in [his] mind, with great anxiety," wished for David Wedderburn's advice, but finally decided that Pitt's maxim was a good one: "When people are disposed to quarrel with you, the best way is to prevent them."[97] On June

[95] Monberaut to Johnstone, June 19, 1765 (II), Gage Papers.

[96] *Ibid.*

[97] The reference is to the Great Commoner's proposal to attack Spain in 1761 in order to "prevent" or interdict a Spanish attack upon Great Britain.

26, he replied to Monberaut's "long, vain, tedious, puffing Memorial."

Taking time only to put the deputy superintendent in the worst possible light, the governor did not long leave him in suspense as to his status in the province.

> I shall now propose two things for your consideration— The first is, to come and reside at Pensacola till your affairs in West Florida can be finished, & to embark in three days from the receipt of this letter. The other is, to embark in four days for New Orleans. Otherwise I have issued a warrant to take you into custody as a man suspected of carrying on schemes destructive to the government and your process shall be regularly made. . . . In the meanwhile I suspend you from all the cares of the Indians, which have so much oppressed you for the seven days you have had the charge, or any transaction with them of any kind whatsoever. . . .[98]

Having abrogated the original agreement, the governor set forth new regulations by which the Chevalier was to conduct himself. Relative to his personal affairs in British West Florida, Monberaut was graciously permitted all the time he needed if he wished to settle them personally, but during that time Johnstone required that he reside at Pensacola. If he appointed someone else to act as his agent, that person would be allowed four months to complete any transactions, provided he took the oath of fidelity to the British Crown during that time. Anyone who wished to follow Monberaut's fortunes, except his children and his two white servants, must leave the province in one month or take the oath of allegiance to George III.[99]

Certain that Monberaut's letter was "calculated for more distant ends, by laying a basis for a second means how to deceive others," Johnstone proceeded to answer every paragraph with more acrimony than accuracy. As the governor explained to Colonel Wedderburn, "The reason of my writing with so much gall, & indeed somewhat impolite, is to throw a perfect ridicule on his character in case he goes to claim a merit at another court." To Wedderburn also went warrants for the arrest of both Monberaut and Favre and

[98] Johnstone to Monberaut, June 26, 1765, Gage Papers.
[99] MJ, pp. 37-51 (95-104); Colonial Office 5/72: 127-142.

the advice to serve the warrants simultaneously in order "to strike both with more astonishment."[100]

The governor's letter reached Monberaut at noon on Saturday, July 6. As Wedderburn was prostrated by fever, delivery was made "avec grande formalité" by Lieutenant Robert Lindsay of the 22nd Regiment. Wedderburn obviously declined to act with the violence Johnstone intended and, alone among the officials of West Florida, retained Monberaut's friendship and respect.[101] The tenor of the letter was nonetheless clear, and Monberaut's first inclination was to go to Pensacola in order to defend himself before his accuser and let the provincial council judge his case. On closer consideration he realized how much militated against his success. The governor was at the height of his power, and the council, dominated by Johnstone's appointees, could be expected to support the governor. Even the running dispute between Johnstone and the military had been settled for the moment through the intervention of Colonel Wedderburn.[102] Monberaut's own popularity with the Indians might cause a demonstration in his behalf, but that would only support the accusation that he was endeavoring to keep up a French party among the savages.

Persuaded that Johnstone meant to ruin him and fearful that confiscation of his property would result from his failure to obey the governor's orders, Monberaut satisfied his conscience for the moment by writing to the two legal officers of the colony, Chief Justice William Clifton and Attorney General Edmund Rush Wegg (both of whom were bitter political opponents of the governor), asking their aid and assistance in his affairs and promising to pre-

[100] Johnstone to Wedderburn, June 27, 1765, Gage Papers. Favre was duly arrested and so ill-treated that his case was cited to the Board of Trade as an example of those "numerous Grievances we have hitherto laboured under from the Administration of Governor Johnstone." It appears that Favre was arrested in June by Wedderburn, confined in the guard room at Mobile until September, and then sent to Pensacola where he was held in the governor's house for several days. *MPAED,* I, 303-305.

[101] See Monberaut's letters to the Chief Justice and Attorney General, July 8, 1765, and to Wedderburn, July 29, 1765, Colonial Office 5/71: 301-303, and Colonial Office 5/72: 147-149.

[102] Rea, "Outpost of Empire," p. 227.

sent his case in full at some happier future date.[103] Making the hastiest dispositions for the sale of his properties and leaving the details to the merchant William Irving, Monberaut departed for New Orleans where, in a position of relative safety, he hoped to exonerate himself from the "false and calumnious imputations" of the British governor.[104]

Safely established beyond Johnstone's reach by July 29, Monberaut advised Colonel Wedderburn, upon whose evidence he hoped to refute Johnstone's charges, that although he had encountered some hostility at New Orleans because of his willingness to serve the king of England, no one was surprised by the treatment he had received from Johnstone, and all were inclined to believe in his innocence.[105] Commandant Aubry put it quite succinctly when he advised John Stuart that "Monsieur de Monberaut . . . does not appear to be extremely satisfied with *messieurs les Anglois* nor with their government."[106]

To add injury to insult, Monberaut encountered complete frustration in attempting to dispose of his property in West Florida. Because of his rapid departure he had had to sell all his goods on credit as well as at far less than their real value. Lisloy went for nothing to the purchaser of its herds in order that the sale might be completed. The plantation on the Choctaw River was sold for £1,200, less costs; the crops, which were ready to be harvested, brought twice that sum to the purchasers. Monberaut's houses in Mobile were a complete loss, and his lot in Pensacola was transferred to the neighboring blacksmith, George Wisnar, without any evident consideration for Monberaut's legal rights.[107]

After some time had passed, the Chevalier dispatched Louis

[103] Monberaut to the Chief Justice and Attorney General, July 8, 1765, Colonial Office 5/71: 301-303. Hamilton dates this letter July 10.

[104] MJ, p. 71 (118); Johnstone to Stuart, July 16, 1765; Wedderburn to Gage, July 24, 1765, Gage Papers. Monberaut considered his date of separation to be July 10, and subsequently asked for his pension as from that date. "MPAED," MS IV, 331-337.

[105] Monberaut to [Wedderburn], New Orleans, July 29, 1765, Colonial Office 5/72: 147-149.

[106] Aubry to Stuart, September 1, 1765, Gage Papers.

[107] Monberaut's "Etat des Biens," Colonial Office 5/71: 303; Howard, *British West Florida*, p. 69.

Augustin to Mobile to secure the payment due from the agent William Irving. Instead of meeting his obligations, Irving attempted to have young Montaut arrested on the ground that he had been sent to West Florida to stir up the Indians against the British. Louis Augustin learned of this breach of faith and avoided arrest; he was even able to confront Irving with his duplicity, but the agent callously advised Montaut that under the circumstances discretion lay in flight, and Monberaut's son returned to New Orleans empty-handed. Irving's authority to act for the Frenchman was promptly revoked, but his successor, Daniel Ward, proved no more helpful in securing payment from Monberaut's debtors.[108]

In spite of his efforts, Johnstone was not able to prevent Monberaut's "claiming a credit at another court." The Spaniards subsequently gave him the rank of colonel and made his son a captain.[109] But again, in changing masters, Monberaut made an unfortunate choice. The French inhabitants of Louisiana bitterly opposed the cession of their colony to Spain and, taking advantage of every opportunity to misconstrue the actions of the Spanish governor, Don Antonio de Ulloa, they rose in open revolt in 1768.[110] Monberaut incurred the wrath of the insurgents by attempting to dissuade them from their dangerous determination to remain French and by undertaking, even at the risk of his life, to return them to their duty. Ulloa was ultimately forced to depart for Havana, and Monberaut, fearing total financial ruin, began to salvage what he could of his estate so that he could embark his family on the first available ship bound for France.[111]

108 Monberaut's "Notes instructives," Colonial Office 5/71: 297-298. Hamilton's account (p. 237) is in error. Louis Augustin did not remain at Mobile, and Monberaut does not accuse Charles Stuart of causing his difficulties. The Chevalier had no love for Charles Stuart, whom he mistakenly believed to be related to John Stuart, but he accused Irving of full responsibility for his son's embarrassment. We have not found the "mémoire justificatif from Montaut, Jr." mentioned by Hamilton.

109 Haldimand to Gage, July 7, 1767; Gage to Shelburne, August 31, 1767, in Clarence E. Carter (ed.) *The Correspondence of General Thomas Gage with the Secretaries of State, 1763-1775* (New Haven, 1931), I, 150.

110 Charles Gayarré, *History of Louisiana* (New Orleans, 1903), II, *passim.*

111 Monberaut to Comte de Monberaut, Louisiana, October 31, 1768, Archives du Ministère des Colonies, C13 A, 48: 98-99 (photostatic copies in the

There were some difficulties concerning his passage home, in view of his service with the English, but Aubry's friendship and interest prevailed to secure Monberaut's removal at the king's expense. By August 1769, he and his sons were in France enjoying the generosity of his brother the Comte de Montaut. The Chevalier lost no time in pressing his case at court, and with the count's support, on August 6, 1769, he was granted a pension of 400 livres a year, payable in two equal installments. The pension was still being paid in 1779, when it was renewed by the government of Louis XVI. Apparently Monberaut returned to Cazeres and was still living, still embroiled in financial complications, as late as 1786.[112]

The activities of the former deputy superintendent while in Louisiana aroused little further interest in British West Florida. Governor Johnstone blamed him for inciting the Houmas and Alabamas living beyond the British pale to raid Fort Butte in 1765, but Aubry's investigation, as might have been expected, disclosed nothing to support the governor's allegations.[113] In the summer of 1767, Brigadier General Frederick Haldimand suggested that Monberaut might yet be worth having, but there was hardly any reason for General Gage's renewed concern that "some mischief is apprehended from that Person's resentment and influence over the savages."[114]

Library of Congress, Washington, D. C.). On May 29, 1769 Joseph de Palacios petitioned for relief from confinement at the suit of the Chevalier who had lately removed from New Orleans to France. James A. Padgett (ed.), "Minutes of the West Florida Assembly," *Louisiana Historical Quarterly,* XXIII (1940), pp. 55-56.

112 Archives de France, Marine C7, p. 215; La Chenaye-Desbois et Badier, *Dictionnaire de la Noblesse,* IV, 89-90.

113 Stuart to Gage, January 11, 1766, Gage Papers. The little post at the juncture of the Iberville and the Mississippi was raided by fifty Indians on August 27, 1765. Engineer Archibald Robertson, unable to save a thing, fled to New Orleans. See the letter from Robertson to Gage, September 2, 1765; Robertson to Bouquet, September 4, 1765, Gage papers. Also see Robert R. Rea, "A Naval Visitor in British West Florida," *Florida Historical Quarterly,* XL (1961), 142-153.

114 Haldimand to Gage, July 7, 1765, Gage Papers; Gage to Shelburne, August 31, 1767, in Carter, *Correspondence,* I, 150.

L'affaire Monberaut dragged out for several years, however, thanks to the persistence of its principal and extensive delays inherent in British colonial administration and eighteenth century communication. Action against Monberaut had been taken by Governor Johnstone on his own initiative, and not until August, 1765, did John Stuart, by then at Charlestown, receive word of his deputy's dismissal. The superintendent promptly decided against any intervention on Monberaut's behalf in spite of once having had "Expectations of Assistance from him [that] were pretty high." Monberaut had been given written instructions, and if he had overstepped his authority Stuart would assume no further responsibility; in fact, he was ready to attribute any difficulty to a fatal flaw in his agent's character: "Mons. Monberaut's ruling passion is avarice; when a dollar was to be got, his Vanity & Grandeur grovelled in the dirt." Stuart agreed with the governor that such a man could not be left in control of Indian affairs.[115]

Monberaut's next line of defense lay with General Gage in New York. He looked upon Gage as his patron (a view shared by Stuart) and appealed to him for fulfillment of his claims. The general replied that he could do nothing about Monberaut's dismissal, and he forwarded the Frenchman's accounts to John Stuart at Charlestown.[116] Stuart denied any financial obligations to Monberaut and observed that £250 had already been given to his former deputy. This he considered sufficient for a man he had caught in many fraudulent practices. Gage agreed that Monberaut had been "very well paid."[117]

After his return to France, Monberaut appealed directly to the British government. He appears to have submitted a memorial in 1769 and again in 1770 when he approached the government through the French minister, M. Frances. In neither case was he successful. The Earl of Hillsborough, Secretary of State for the

[115] Stuart to Gage, August 30, 1765, Colonial Office 5/72: 113-116.

[116] MJ, p. 7 (77); Gage to Stuart, February 26, 1767, Colonial Office 5/72: 151-152. According to Hamilton, Monberaut wrote to Gage in September 1765, but the letter does not appear in the Gage Papers.

[117] Stuart to Gage, March 24, 1767, and Gage to Stuart, May 8, 1767, Colonial Office 5/72: 153-161.

Colonies, merely expressed his regret that an employee of the Crown should feel justified in complaining of his treatment. He did promise to make "the fullest Inquiry," however, and promptly forwarded Monberaut's claims to Stuart for adjudication. No more effective conclusion of the case could have been found, for in his latest "Mémoire" the Frenchman had placed most of the blame for his misfortune upon the superintendent and had excused Johnstone as a dupe, trapped by his "humeur feroce" into serving Stuart's purposes. Stuart castigated the memorial as "a most indecent, illiberal, & scurrilous performance" and rejected every claim. There the matter rested—officially and finally.[118]

That his cause should be unheard, his expenses unrequited, was due to no negligence on the part of Montault de Monberaut. Hurrying to New Orleans to escape Johnstone's wrath, he had begun the preparation of a fulsome address to George III, his ministers, and all who might wish to see justice done. Unfortunately he had contracted a debilitating illness—"an infection of the ears which was followed by violent headaches which lasted a very long time"—and until February 1, 1766, he was unable to write more than a brief appeal to General Thomas Gage.[119] The labors of the winter, however, produced the lengthy document entitled "Mémoire Justificatif de M. Le Chevalier De Montault de Monberaut en sa qualité de Député Superintendant pour les affaires relatives aux Indiens dans la province D'West Florida. Le dit Mémoire servant de Refutation et Réponse, aux imputations fausses et calomnieuses que luy a fait Mr. George Johnstone, Governeur de la ditte province D'West Florida." Although its author claimed no talent save that inspired by outraged virtue, the "Mémoire Justificatif" is not lacking in literary merit. Its true value, however, lies in the minute details through which the Frenchman's career may be studied, for he included most of the correspondence which passed between himself and the British officials and chronicled

118 "MPAED," MS IV, 331-337; Hillsborough to Frances, and Hillsborough to Stuart, July 31, 1770, Colonial Office 5/71: 285, 289; Stuart to Hillsborough, November 29, 1770, Colonial Office 5/72: 85-95.

119 The manuscript in the Gage Papers bears the date February 1, 1766; Hamilton, p. 236, dates it November 17, 1766.

the events which transpired during his brief tenure. No other single document holds such a wealth of information concerning the Indian affairs of British West Florida or fills so many gaps in the official records.

In spite of his efforts to throw the blame for any illogical order on the governor, the "Mémoire" was based upon the points that Monberaut himself had raised in his second memorandum to Johnstone and Stuart, June 19, 1765, for in his reply the governor had simply denounced each of the seventeen articles of the Chevalier's letter. The "Mémoire" proved the insulted Frenchman to be as adept in the art of snide insinuation, plain and fancy insult, as his antagonist, and even more long-winded! Extracted from all the vituperation and rhetoric, the essence of the controversy lay in Johnstone's charges that Monberaut was disloyal to the British Crown and wasteful of government funds. His guilt, the governor averred, relieved the colony of its contractual obligations.

Johnstone sought to leave the Frenchman no defense against the charge of extravagance; from the very outset the British had insisted on the need for strict economy, yet Monberaut had tried to extort £8 per day from Stuart while the superintendent lodged with him at Mobile.[120] The erstwhile deputy's lack of concern for the straitened circumstances of the colony was further evidenced by his unreasonable desire to continue the French practice of feeding the savages and keeping them pacified with gifts. To these charges the Chevalier replied that there was no question of expenses prior to completion of the congresses, and that, in addition, the practice of giving presents to the Indians was not only effective but a practical necessity.

More serious was the governor's accusation that the Chevalier had tried to maintain a pro-French party in the Choctaw Nation and had created obstacles to a peaceful settlement with the Creeks. As evidence Johnstone pointed out that Monberaut's speech to

[120] Stuart later declared, "I altered my lodging much for the worse to a large old house without a pen [sic] of glass. . . . I submit that the Superintendent had a good right to lodge in a house hired for the service of his own Department at the rate of £100 Sterling pr anno £50 of which were actually paid." Stuart to Hillsborough, November 29, 1770, Colonial Office 5/72: 85-95.

the Choctaws was so inappropriate that he had had to alter it before he could allow it to be made. Monberaut retorted that in only three places had the governor seen fit to revise the harangue, and those changes were inconsequential.

Johnstone dwelt at length upon affairs concerning The Mortar with whom, he alleged, the Frenchman had had no influence. His only service had been in knowing where to find Topalga and using him to locate the Creek chieftain. As for persuading him to come to Pensacola, Johnstone claimed that The Mortar gave the credit to William Struthers.

In the official report of the Pensacola congress, The Mortar had been quoted as stating that Monberaut was responsible for the settlement of the boundary dispute, but the governor was unwilling to admit it. Johnstone confessed to having seen the Creeks yield to the Chevalier's representations, but, he added, that was no wonder as Monberaut was both the author and dispeller of their alarms, "allways ready to deliver the mountain of a mouse and to magnify a mouse into a mountain."

Monberaut's version of the participation of William Struthers in the Creek congress differed drastically. He claimed that when Struthers offered his services to the colony, the governor turned him off saying, "I do not seek . . . any service from you; I only ask you not to traverse the operations of the people we have sent." Moreover, The Mortar had declared in front of witnesses that had it not been for Monberaut's letter and the sight of Louis Augustin, he would never have come to Pensacola. The Chevalier further cited an old trader in the town of Pakanatalisi, "a man well versed in Indian politics," who attested that the Sieur de Montaut's demeanor and the prestige of his father's name were the decisive factors in persuading The Mortar to journey to the capital. The old man added that the Chevalier and his son had accomplished more with three rolls of tobacco than any Englishman could have done with fifty pieces of Limbourg.[121]

Against the younger Montauts Johnstone launched some of his most vicious sarcasm. He described Louis Augustin as ". . . a boy,

[121] Limbourg was the staple cloth of the Indian trade.

very much spoiled by the natural disposition of his mind and by the haughty puffs and low intrigues of his acquaintance." "I have had some little trouble in Saving your son from a very vexatious prosecution, that of Horse stealing." Of the younger son he wrote, "I believe it can be proved . . . that the publick bread was sold by your own family through the Streets of Mobile."

The haughty Chevalier was no less quick to respond to insult to his sons than to himself or his ancestors. The accusation of selling bread "astonished" Monberaut, but not so much that he was unable to reply. The only family he had had with him in Mobile was a thirteen-and-a-half-year-old lad who might have bartered bread to the Indians for bows and arrows, but if Stuart had reported it, a few strokes of the parental whip would have put an end to that affair.

As for Louis Augustin's acquaintance being given to "low intrigues," that obviously referred to Louis Forneret, whom Johnstone had disparagingly portrayed as a soldier who wrote a good hand, spelled better than a Frenchman should, had married a "pretty woman, [and] by a pretty puff his mind is allways on the fret." Monberaut observed that Forneret doubtless had very good reasons to be upset, because Johnstone was probably trying to seduce his wife![122]

In reply to the accusation that Montaut was a horse thief, his father offered an exculpatory letter from the notorious horse thief and swindler, James Noble—a remarkably weak prop on which to rest his case.

Thus did the Chevalier technically refute every charge made

[122] This rather intriguing suggestion is supported after a fashion by the Anglican itinerant Charles Woodmason, who visited West Florida in 1765: "The Governour is a Single Person, keeps a Concubine, has a Child by her and the Infection rages, and is copied" (Richard J. Hooker [ed.], *The Carolina Backcountry on the Eve of the Revolution* [Chapel Hill, 1953], p. 82). It may be noted that Mme. Forneret was granted 150 acres on Bonsecour River on October 3, 1766, and Louis Forneret received a separate 125-acre grant in the same area December 18, 1767 (Howard, *British West Florida*, pp. 77, 85). Louis Forneret may be identified with that Louis Fornent of Mobile who manumitted his Negro woman Mary and their three mulatto children and provided them with a herd of cattle. See Cecil Johnson, *British West Florida 1763-1783* (New Haven, 1943), p. 178.

against him by the governor. Copying verbatim the correspondence which he had meticulously saved, he named witnesses to his actions and asked that they be questioned under oath to prove the facts set forth in the "Mémoire Justificatif." The presentation of his case far surpassed that of the irate governor, who contradicted himself, admitted his ignorance of the facts, and packed his charges with calculated lies. But Johnstone had the advantage of striking the first blow, and in the circles of those who might judge them, the royal governor's word must surely have been expected to carry more weight than that of a disgruntled Gallic mercenary.

Monberaut conceived three possible explanations for the governor's hostile action. First, he suggested jealousy of his increasing influence with the savages. His success in treating with the Indians might have gained him more renown than was enjoyed by the officials charged with that responsibility in the colony. Of this he need not have been fearful; the official reports gave him scant notice. Second, he felt that upon the successful completion of the two congresses his service and advice were no longer needed. John Stuart later took the line that Indian affairs had not really been so bad in 1765, and he had never expected Johnstone to continue Monberaut's employment.[123] Perhaps not, but the governor clearly expected his action against Monberaut to come as a surprise to the superintendent and took pains to express his hope "as we have hitherto constantly agreed, that we shall not differ on this point."[124] In truth, none knew better than the Chevalier that he had done all that a Frenchman could to aid the British in West Florida.

In light of subsequent events, perhaps the provocation lay in the third point—the counter-allegation that Johnstone was disappointed by the maintenance of peace. The governor had remarked to Monberaut that "his greatest interest could be found in the greatest trouble in the province under his command" for there was great profit to be made in an Indian war. At first Monberaut had thought much credit due to a governor who nobly set aside his personal advantage for the good of a few subjects, but he seems to

123 Stuart to Hillsborough, November 29, 1770, Colonial Office 5/72: 85-95.

124 Johnstone to Stuart, July 16, 1765, Gage Papers.

have convinced himself that the governor dismissed him in the hope that he might provide a *casus belli.* Johnstone was certainly aware that Monberaut's intrigues might occasion "some little fracas" and to Stuart the governor wrote of "publick declarations that he would undo all we had done"—a threat (if made) that could not be ignored.[125] The sting of Monberaut's apparently fantastic charge lies in the fact that it was Johnstone's belligerent policy toward the Creeks in 1766, almost precipitating war, that brought about his recall by the British government.[126]

West Florida survived in spite of Indian alarms and endless bickering between successive governors and colonists until the tide of revolution swept down the continent and Spain returned to rule the coast. Happily the iron-bound chests and boxes which held the military papers of General Thomas Gage survived the holocaust. Conveyed to safety overseas, they made the crossing westward once again and are now located in the great manuscript collection of the William L. Clements Library. There Monberaut's "Mémoire Justificatif" lies in fitting company with reports, petitions, merchants' bills, and plaints of fever-ridden redcoats far from home, part of the outpouring of a growing empire and a nation struggling to be born.

[125] Johnstone to Wedderburn, June 27, 1765, and Johnstone to Stuart, July 16, 1765, Gage Papers.

[126] Shelburne to Gage, February 19, 1767, Carter, *Correspondence,* II, 51.

A Note on the Sources

ANY STUDY OF THE history of British West Florida or of the career of Montault de Monberaut must be based upon the papers of General Thomas Gage which are held by the William L. Clements Library, Ann Arbor, Michigan. This great manuscript collection contains Gage's correspondence with Governor George Johnstone, Superintendent John Stuart, Monberaut, Lieutenant Colonel David Wedderburn and those British army officers who were the founders and defenders of the colony. Official though it was, the peculiarities of eighteenth century military correspondence allowed great room for personality to express itself, and this collection provides the only intimate glimpse of the formative period in British West Florida. The small portion of the Gage papers published by Clarence E. Carter, *The Correspondence of General Thomas Gage with the Secretaries of State, 1763-1775* (New Haven, 1931), barely suggests the riches of the collection. The Wedderburn papers, also in the William L. Clements Library, contain a few private letters from the commanding officer of the 22nd Regiment at Mobile which have been utilized by Robert Rea in "Outpost of Empire: David Wedderburn at Mobile," *Alabama Review*, VII (1954).

The British Colonial Office papers in the Public Record Office in London are also of great value. Photostatic copies of these manuscripts, which are held by the Library of Congress Manuscripts Division, Washington, D.C., have been used for this study. Extensive transcripts of these and other British manuscripts were made for Dunbar Rowland and the Mississippi State Department of Archives and History, Jackson, Mississippi. Rowland edited and published only one volume of this collection, *Mississippi Provincial Archives, 1763-1766. English Dominion,* I (Nashville, 1911). The unpublished transcripts in the collection have also been consulted for this study. Some further transcripts of British material are held by the Alabama State Department of Archives and History, Montgomery, Alabama. The Archives de France, Paris, contain a few documents relating to Monberaut which have served to establish the chronology of his life. The most important item is a hitherto unnoticed dossier from the Department de la Marine which is not to be found among the French Transcripts in the Library of Congress. Daniel H. Thomas, "Fort Toulouse: The French Outpost at the Alibamos on the Coosa," *Alabama Historical Quarterly,* XXII (1960), is the most thorough study on the French side.

Jean-Bernard Bossu's *Nouveaux Voyages aux Indies Occidentales* (Paris, 1768), is the only contemporary publication to shed any light upon the personality and activity of Monberaut. It has been translated and edited by Seymour Feiler as *Jean-Bernard Bossu's Travels in the Interior of North America 1751-1762* (Norman, Okla., 1962). On the British colonial side the most interesting observations are those published by Wilbur R. Jacobs, *Indians of the Southern Colonial Frontier: The Edmond Atkin Report and the Plan of 1755* (Columbia, S. C., 1954).

The most noteworthy of the older studies of British West Florida is Peter J. Hamilton's *Colonial Mobile* (New York, 1897, rev. 1910, reissued Mobile, 1952). Hamilton drew upon previously untapped British and French manuscript sources; his chapter on Monberaut was based upon a transcript of the Chevalier's "Mémoire," but he was unable to refer to the most important British correspondence (see Henry P. Beers, *The French in North America* [Baton Rouge, 1957], p. 126). The surviving Hamilton transcripts were located by Milo B. Howard in 1961 at the State Department of Archives and History, Montgomery, Alabama.

Three modern scholars have done much to clear the brush from about the roots of British West Florida. Clinton N. Howard's research, originally scattered in article form, is largely gathered together in *The Development of British West Florida 1763-1769*, (University of California Publications in History, XXXIV [Berkeley, 1947]), which provides much illuminating information concerning property interests in the colony. Cecil Johnson, *British West Florida 1763-1783* (New Haven, 1943), is the only complete study of the province and makes use of the Gage papers. John R. Alden's study of Indian policy, *John Stuart and the Southern Colonial Frontier* (Ann Arbor, 1944), is similarly dependent upon the William L. Clements Library manuscripts and provides the most valuable supplement to this present work, whose authors must insist that Monberaut's contribution to the settlement of Indian affairs was considerably greater than the superintendent's biographer allows.

The Mémoire Justificatif
of the Chevalier Montault de Monberaut

Letter to the King of England

SIRE

The rare qualities with which Your Majesty is endowed, and above all your love of justice, inspire in me the great confidence with which I address myself to Your Majesty, begging you to stretch out to me a helping hand and make my innocence triumph over the false imputations which Mr. George Johnstone, Governor of West Florida, has made against me.

Passing over the force which you could employ to overcome the savages, approving only methods which the goodness of your heart dictated to you for gaining them, Your Majesty charged Governor Johnstone and Mr. John Stuart to win them over to your interests, ordering them to make your clemency more to be admired by the Nations than your power to be dreaded.

Those two gentlemen, obliged to conform to the orders dictated by such glorious sentiments, found no means more efficacious than to attach to Your Majesty's service and to your crown those who were known to be esteemed among those Nations, and being informed of the credit which I had and that I knew the politics of the Indians, they thought me useful to their operations and eagerly sought me out, giving every evidence of a respect and an affection which they were far from having in their hearts.

His Excellency, the Right Honorable Major General Gage, commanding Your Majesty's forces in America, had sought me out before they did on the report that Mr. Robertson, Quartermaster General of Your Majesty's said army, had made to him concerning the mastery which he himself had recognized that I had of the mentality of the savage Nations.

As General Gage in his letter of invitation pointed out to me, he feared that, in view of the profession I made of the Catholic, Apostolic, and Roman religion, I was myself an obstacle to the good disposition which he had in my favor. In my replies to His Excellency, I told him without evasion that the most flattering prospects, the most eminent employment, and the most considerable advantages were not capable of altering my belief in regard to the fundamental points of my religion.

I replied to the first overtures of Messrs. Johnstone and Stuart only by showing them His Excellency General Gage's letters which observed with rectitude that the profession of my religion prohibited me from any type of employment by England.

Governor Johnstone and Superintendent Stuart, not being able to gainsay the truth of that which General Gage said, sought evasions and exceptions to the law made in England against Catholics and consequently offered me the position of Deputy Superintendent for Indian Affairs in West Florida, which employment (they said) was not subject to the law made against Catholics.

I shall not bore Your Majesty, Sire, by detailing all that has passed in my negotiations with Messrs. Johnstone and Stuart; they have been lengthy. I will summarize by saying to Your Majesty that those gentlemen established the propositions they made me in writing, to which I made my observations in writing and set forth my conditions in turn.

The facility with which they granted me, in writing, generally all the points of the agreement[*] which I made, caused me to accept with confidence the commission of Deputy Superintendent of Indian Affairs for the Province of West Florida, which they gave me while awaiting the same commission issued directly by Your Majesty, as those gentlemen promised me.

In the position which had been given me I rendered to Your Majesty, Sire, and to the state, every possible service. In order to prove that which I advance, I call upon the testimony of Admiral

[*Monberaut uses "capitulation" here—which Johnstone uses in a literal sense. Eds.]

Sir William Burnaby and of the captains and officers of his squadron, especially Captain Carket who did not miss any conference at the Pensacola congress; that of Lieutenant Colonel Wedderburn, attached to the 22nd Regiment. This Lieutenant Colonel was present at all that passed and was negotiated at the two congresses of Mobile and Pensacola, and as he speaks good French, he had the kindness whenever I needed an English interpreter, to explain to them what I had had to say to the savages.

All the notables of the church, of the Law, of the military and civil population attended the sessions of the congress held at Mobile and Pensacola. I also call upon the testimony of the interpreters, English as well as French, and of the traders, resident as well as itinerant, in the savage Nations, particularly those among the Creeks.

I beg Your Majesty, Sire, to order that judicial inquiry be made on this subject to the end that there may be no deception caused either by Mr. Johnstone's report or by mine.

Not only, Sire, have I served Your Majesty in person, but immediately upon my acceptance of the position, I even hazarded my elder son, sending him among the savages to engage their Chiefs to come to attend the proposed congresses. Those chiefs were, for the most part, very indisposed toward the English; my son ran some risk if they had ceased having confidence in me, and at their arrival, they did not hide the fact that they were determined to come solely by my invitation, certified by the embassy of my son.

After the signal services which I have rendered with fidelity and honor, ought I to have expected to be treated by Mr. Johnstone as a traitor, thief and grafter? Such are the names which he gives me in depriving me of my employment and denying me the fulfillment of the conditions which I stipulated in my agreement with him and Mr. Stuart. Will he say that an employment of that nature cannot be entrusted to a Catholic who has not taken the oath as a subject? An allegation like that on his part must seem frivolous. These two articles, and that in which I demand that, in case I am put out of employment, he would allow me a pension of one half of my salary, payable any place where I might establish myself, are the three principles of the agreement that he accorded me.

I had to make these reservations for fear that Your Majesty or your ministers would not approve a Catholic and a foreigner holding that position, and in that case, not having confirmed my status by any oath, I could return to my previous condition as subject and sometime servant of the King of France. I would sacrifice time too precious for my fortune and that of my family not to seek to be indemnified for the loss of that which I used. That is the motive which made me demand a pension.

I do not believe that such foresight could appear blamable in view of the fact that I had deferred my entire determination as to allegiance until Your Majesty had made known your intention in my regard.

In the length of time that Messrs. Johnstone and Stuart have treated with me, they ought to have known if it was or was not in their power to grant my demands. If they had refused me, I should have seen what I had to do, and Mr. Johnstone would not have needed to have recourse to the infamous extremity of suspecting me of crimes which I am incapable of committing.

In the afflicting circumstances in which I find myself, I have recourse, Sire, to Your Majesty, whom I beg to have pity on the state to which I am reduced. *They have attacked my honor and have effectively ruined me.*

I dare to hope, Sire, that Your Majesty will order that reparations be made to my honor, indemnities be given for the losses which I have been occasioned in my goods, and that a pension will be allowed me, like that which has been accorded me in the agreement which Messrs. Stuart and Johnstone have made with me.

I beg Your Majesty, Sire, to permit me to represent to you that I am not a vagabond running from kingdom to kingdom with a view to extorting a job. I am a French gentleman, born of a house which holds distinguished rank in its province, allied to families of more illustrious birth than mine. I have had the honor of serving the King of France for the space of twenty-six years, and I have honorable certificates of commendation from the commandants under whose orders I have served. Mr. Johnstone, who has seen them as well as my genealogy, far from being held back by those considerations, bases an article of reproach on them, treating as froth this sort of document which the rest of the world finds honorable.

I cannot be reproached for having been a traitor to the King of France, of whom I am a native subject and have been a servant; *I was no longer employed by him,* and the article of the treaty by which Mobile was ceded to England allowed me to choose the master under whose domination I wished to live.

My misfortune came, Sire, from the circumstances which rendered me the possessor of property in the territory of Mobile ceded to Your Majesty. I had sold this property to Mr. Jones who bought it for and in the name of Admiral Sir William Burnaby. W. G. Blackwell, Collector, was to have paid me; so he had promised. Only Mr. Johnstone's arrival at Mobile made him change his mind, and I do not hesitate to advance that it is Mr. Johnstone who has dissuaded Mr. Blackwell from making that payment, for he told me several times that he did in that matter only what the Governor counseled. That change on the part of the Collector put me under the necessity of taking back my property. Probably Mr. Johnstone only persuaded Mr. Blackwell not to advance that sum for the Admiral with the design of catching me in his web.

Being thus reduced to the alternative of losing my possessions or changing allegiance, it is not astonishing that I accepted a position which could procure me considerations equivalent to those which I had in my native country, which I loved and only quitted under duress and with regret.

I have the honor, Sire, to assure Your Majesty that, notwithstanding my patriotic devotion, I have not ceased, during all the time I have been employed, to serve Your Majesty and the state with fidelity, zeal, integrity, and honor. I have had the satisfaction of seeing my operations crowned by success; my persuasion, more than that of him who was supposed to, has determined the savages to submit voluntarily to Your Majesty's dominion; for although Mr. Stuart, Superintendent-in-Chief, to whom I was only Deputy, had been imprisoned by the Cherokees, I am not convinced that his knowledge in the polity of the savages was superior to mine. The lessons which he has received from his teachers, the Cherokees, are not better than those which my children and friends the Alabamas, Abihkas, Tallapoosas, Cowetas, Kashitas, Conchatys, Chouanons, Choctaws, Chakchiumas, Houmas, Bayogoulas, Ofogoulas, Avoyels, Tunicas, Ougappas, Pascagoulas, Taensaws, Chatots, &c. have given to me—and even the Cherokees, teachers of Mr. Stuart, who is not ignorant that by winning them to the French side, I forged the first links of the chain which bound him.*

The great confidence which the vast majority of the savages showed me and the honors which they rendered me, and which they were far from giving and having for Mr. Stuart, gave birth to the jealousy which induced him to work for my ruin. He was very well seconded by Governor Johnstone who, although too wickedly cunning to be able to hope to see attributed to himself any part of an honor of which he wished to deprive me, debased himself to the point of having recourse to the imposture of diverting to Mr. Stuart some of the glory which was due me for the success of the negotiations with the savages; and he dares maliciously to tax me with treason &c.

It is the falsehood of similar imputations, also wickedly concocted, which has forced me, Sire, to address to Your Majesty a memorial which contains all that has passed since the moment when Mr. Stuart and Johnstone sought me out until that at which I received the defamatory arrêt by which Mr. Johnstone deprives me of my employment.

I would be overjoyed if Your Majesty deigned to look at the report contained in my Memorial; you would know the true sentiments of the savages and could not doubt the right I have of asking the reparations due my honor and the execution of the articles of

* I commanded at the post of the Alabamas from 1755 until the month of May 1759. When I took possession of my command, the Cherokees were allies of the English and made war on the French and on the Alabamas, their allies. I not only negotiated the peace which the French and the Alabamas made with the Cherokees, but I persuaded that nation away from the English alliance and laid the first foundations of the sanguinary war that they made on them; that is why I rightly say that I forged the first links of the chain that bound Mr. Stuart.

the agreement which had been accorded me. That agreement, in the form of a letter, is one of the pieces contained in my Memorial which justifies me on every point of Mr. Johnstone's false accusations and proves that it was not even probable, and that it would have been necessary that I had totally lost my judgment if, without hope of being granted any recompense, I had wished, beginning a service under a new allegiance, to ruin myself in my possessions and in my honor for the sole satisfaction of being a traitor.

One does not come all at once to that excess of crime, and my conduct, at all times irreproachable and known to Mr. Johnstone, ought to protect me from an imputation however black.

That Governor is no better founded when he taxes me with having dissipated the funds of Great Britain to satisfy my avarice. To him and Mr. Stuart alone are the funds entrusted, nothing having been in my hands. They would be fortunate if their hands were as clean of the funds of the state as mine are.

I beg Your Majesty, Sire, to believe that it is not from vanity that I have written the advantageous things about myself which are reproduced in this letter and in my memorial. Mr. Johnstone, accusing me of counterfeited crimes, has put me in need of being my own apologist and of trying to make myself known to Your Majesty for what I am. Truth alone can bring to light the falsehood of his imputations, and it is that which I place before Your Majesty. I do not fear being contradicted; at least it will ease me to disclose the imposture.

I dare to hope, Sire, that Your Majesty, recognizing the sentiments of honor and probity which have always guided me, will disapprove the iniquitous proceedings of Mr. Johnstone, and that without examining whether or not I am declared a subject, the title of servant of Your Majesty will suffice in order that you may judge me worthy of your good will and the benefit of your justice. My hope is great, being assured that Your Majesty will be too jealous of your glory, and of what posterity would say, to leave unpunished this governor who, clothed with an authority which Your Majesty had confided to him in order to make your justice admired by protecting the virtuous, had abused it in order, under calumnious pretexts, to oppress a faithful servant of Your Majesty and the state in his possessions and in his honor.

I am, Sire, with the most profound respect,

Your Majesty's
Most humble
And most obedient
Servant
The Chevalier de Montault de Monberaut

Monberaut's Preface

As NOTHING CAN be more humiliating for an honest man than to see himself obliged to justify a conduct which he has had care to direct by the purest sentiments of honor, his satisfaction and his triumph ought to be great when he can prove that the imputations that are made against him are calumnious and full of impostures.

Animated by such flattering hopes, I bring to light a memorial which will make known to those who wish to take the trouble to read it, that Mr. Johnstone, Governor for His Britannic Majesty in the Province of West Florida, has employed means full of iniquity, suggested by the blackest jealousy, for my ruin.

The Governor is without any respect, regard, or consideration

1st for my status as a gentleman allied to the better houses of the Kingdom of France, among which there are even alliances with the reigning house. I speak of this in my memorial in the article by which I reply to the reproach which he makes against me for having shown him a genealogy going back as far as Adam.

2nd He cannot be unaware that I have been a Captain in the service of the King of France, whom I have served with honor, zeal and fidelity,* which he has seen by the certificates that I have shown him which I have had from the governors and commandants

* During the time I was in the service of France, I commanded for more than four years in a frontier fort. Messrs. Johnstone and Stuart have seen the praises which have been given me on my command by the Governor of the Province and the King's Lieutenant Commandant at Mobile.

under whose orders I have served, and from the officers of the corps of which I was a member.

3rd He is wanting in respect for His Excellency General Gage whom he well knows to have sought me out to make me accept employment in the service of England and to have given me marks of his esteem, of his approbation, and offers of his services, if only by informing me that it was beyond his power to satisfy my demands.

4th He has forgotten that he himself and Mr. Stuart, Superintendent for the Indians, sought me out, in writing and verbally, with demonstrations of respect which confuse me.

All these considerations ought to have rendered Mr. Johnstone more circumspect and prevented him from serving me with a defamatory arrêt—without having observed any formality—in the form of a letter full of every imaginable injury.

If Mr. Johnstone had given himself time for reflection it would be easy for him to foresee that his accusations being entirely calumnious, I would not rest in condemnable inaction, especially being able to prove the falsity of his charges.

I have the honor of addressing this justifying memorial to His Britannic Majesty or to his Ministers, begging them to extend to me a helping hand, to give me the means of making my oppressed innocence triumph over the iniquity of a man who has abused an authority placed in his hands for a better use.

As the effects produced by Mr. Johnstone's iniquity have been public, as well as the calumnious imputations on which he based his arrêt, I will make public my justifications, to prove that he who has sought to dishonor me is himself dishonored *ipso facto* by his own unreasonable and calumnious writings.

I am going to set forth, now, the plan upon which my memorial is based.

No one is ignorant that, by the treaty of peace between France and England, Mobile &c. was ceded to England. I had property situated in the territory kept by France; I had some in the territory of Mobile ceded to the English. Not being able to remain subject to two crowns, it was necessary for me to choose in which one of the two places I wished to fix my residence. *I advertised at Mobile that my property was for sale.* In the interval of time which we were granted by the treaty to make our sales, I received on the part of His Excellency General Gage, a letter of invitation to enter His Britannic Majesty's service. I had the honor of responding to His Excellency, establishing for him what conditions of service I would accept. I have inserted in this memorial some fragments of the reply which His Excellency made me. It will be seen in what fashion His Excellency considered my statement.

Mr. Johnstone (having been dispatched by His Britannic Majesty in the capacity of Governor of West Florida) wrote to me immediately upon his arrival and sent Messrs. Maclellan and Charles Stuart to my estate to bring me his letter which I put at the head of my memorial.

The same Mr. Johnstone, Governor, and John Stuart, Superintendent, having come to Mobile, sought to lure me to some conferences on the means of gaining the savages' friendship and concluding a firm and lasting alliance with them. I replied to them that I was French and not engaged in any employment which put me in a position to give them any information, that His Excellency General Gage had already sought me out, and, on my refusal to take up the Anglican religion, had sent me word forthrightly that the profession of my religion was incompatible with the exercise of any employment in England, especially of a military nature.

I note in my memorial the offers that these gentlemen made me in consequence of my response. I make mention of the different conferences that we have had together which were followed by an invitation in writing, which I also put at the head of my memorial. Following Mr. Johnstone's first letter will next be seen the response I made to the letter of invitation from Messrs. Johnstone and Stuart. By that response I established on what conditions I would consent to accept the employment which they proposed to me, that of Deputy Superintendent for all the affairs of the Indians in the Province of West Florida. I place next the Act of Subscription, without any restrictions whatsoever, that Messrs. Johnstone and Stuart made to the propositions which I stipulated. Moreover, it will be seen that what Mr. Johnstone says is wrong when he denies that the conditions whose fulfillment I demand are those which I repeat.

In order that I may have a right to the execution of the agreement that has been made with me, it is necessary that I have merited it by effective and faithful service. This I have done.

Not only the English but even the French have had knowledge of my sentiments on this subject, for in a letter which I wrote to M. Aubry, Commandant of the French troops and, for the interim, of the Province of Louisiana, I have pointed them out to him in one of the paragraphs of that letter by which I give him notification of my acceptance of employment.*

"I believe, Monsieur, that you know me well enough to be persuaded that I will serve the King of England with the same zeal and with the same sentiments of honor and probity which I professed at the time I had the honor of serving the King of France, &c."

If I admit the disagreeable fact that that letter (which has been published at New Orleans) has been generally censured, it provides me the consolation of making it serve as proof against Mr. Johnstone's false imputations. I say more of this in my memorial.

After the Act of Subscription by Messrs. Johnstone and Stuart, a letter went from me to those two gentlemen by which I asked them for an explanation of the talk going about among the people *that I was going to be deprived of my employment,* and, in case such was their intention, I claimed again the execution of the conditions which I had stipulated. That letter, transcribed word for word, is followed by a reply from Mr. Johnstone alone, by which, contrary to all formality, and without even having the right, he dismissed me from my employment and banished me from Mobile, ordering me to leave there in three days if going to Pensacola; but if going to New Orleans, where he indicates I would do well to go, he orders me to leave in four days; and to justify his violent and iniquitous procedure, he has recourse to slander, accusing me of crimes: *1st* of treason, *2nd* of malversation, *3rd* of fraud, for the initial punishment of which he speaks to me with atrocious invective.

That letter, or arrêt (call it what you like, for it is one and the

* The copy of the said letter in its entirety, and certified by M. Aubry, is put at the end of this preface.

same) has ruined me and would indubitably occasion my dishonor if I should leave it without a reply. It was that which put me under the humiliating necessity of drafting a justifying memorial which ought to have been brought to light long since. But having had the misfortune of being attacked upon my arrival at New Orleans by an infection of the ears which was followed by violent headaches which lasted a very long time, I found myself for an interminable time in no condition to work on my justification, and I did not wish to be served by the pen of another. All that I have been able to do, in that great extremity, has been to address myself (a little late, to be sure, but as soon as I was able) to His Excellency the Right Honorable General Gage, asking him not to let himself be taken in by the imposture &c.

I am, therefore, going to expose to the light of day a memorial in which I detail that which has preceded and followed my acceptance in the service of His Britannic Majesty of the position of Deputy Superintendent for all the affairs relative to the Indians in the Province of West Florida.

I prove in my memorial the falsity of Mr. Johnstone's imputations by making him see that not having had any expenditures at my disposal, all of which were made by Mr. Stuart and himself, I had no need to push my intrigues among the interpreters in order to certify my accounts.

In narrating what has passed in the congress and reporting the discourses of the savages, I show that Mr. Johnstone uses deceit when he says that he knew that I did not have any credit among them; I point out the falsity of his accusations when he says that I have sought to corrupt their tender intentions; in fine, I demonstrate clearly that the envy which Mr. Stuart and he have of appropriating to themselves alone the glory of success in the negotiations has suggested to them making the most calumnious charges against me.

In detailing the reasons that I had for furnishing beef for the congress, for sharing my lodging with Mr. Stuart, and for crediting myself for the expense of his table, I prove that Mr. Stuart is an ingrate, false in his charges, in that, first, as to the furnishing of beef, he is not unaware that it was he who earnestly asked me to do it, and that I only did it out of kindness to him.*

Second. As for the expense of his table, he cannot be ignorant that I have expended more than two thousand *piastres* in his behalf and that the three hundred fifty-four *piastres* that he reimbursed me for the total expense of good cheer during nearly three months, for a table serving two and three meals daily for 25 and 30 persons, would hardly be a consideration in order that I might make some profit. Knowing his natural avarice, I have preferred to lose rather than to demand fair reimbursement for the expenses made for the congress, into the details of which a more generous man than he would have insisted upon entering; but Mr. Johnstone and he have concerted to dishonor and ruin me. In depriving me of my honor they count on throwing more luster upon their own operations. In ruining me they have sought to deprive me of every means of justification, knowing well that indigent innocence has trouble in piercing the crowd and presenting itself at the foot of the throne.

I will employ all sorts of means to push mine there. If it has the good fortune of getting there, Messrs. Johnstone and Stuart have everything to fear from the integrity of the Monarch seated on that throne so redoubtable to the guilty.

My memorial is of a length which I perceive might well be boring. That makes me ask the indulgence of the respectable persons to whom it will be presented and of all those who wish to take the trouble to read it. I ask pardon for the narrative, which I myself find dull, but I am not able to help it, considering that it furnishes my justification and proof.

As to the digressions, transgressions, postpositions and omissions, Mr. Johnstone has given me the example; being obliged to follow him step by step, they have become inescapable.

Besides, as I have said above, in a circumstance such as this, I ought to be, I have wished to be, and I think that I could not excuse myself from being the author of my own memorial.

Little versed in the art of literature and totally ignorant of the

* I have inserted in my memorial copies of two letters from Mr. Stuart which will prove that which I advance.

style which justificative memorials ought to have, I have given to mine the form that I have thought suitable in characterizing each section according to its particular attributes.

I hope that the readers will be most willing, in their judgment, to make abstractions of the contour of phrases and of diction and to consider only that I demonstrate that Mr. Johnstone, sustaining in certain places the imputations of the complaints that he says Mr. Stuart has made to him, allows it to be understood that this Mr. Stuart and he are in accord and have together concocted the imputations whose falsity I prove.

My memorial has no other merit than that of being dictated by pure truth. I hope that that spotless virgin, although naked and without arms, will triumph over her enemies, that imposture, calumny and perfidy, although armed at every point, and moreover covered by the shield of authority, will indubitably succumb. This cannot fail to come about under the reign of a prince so just and so enlightened as the one who sits on the throne of England. I therefore implore the justice of the King to condemn Messrs. Johnstone and Stuart to make reparation to my honor, indemnities for my property, of which they have occasioned me loss, and to punish them according to the enormity of their crime.

I dare to flatter myself still further that His Majesty, convinced that I have served him with honor and fidelity, will order that the articles of the agreement which I have made will be executed in every detail, and in consequence will allow me a pension of one hundred five pounds sterling, which pension was promised me when I contracted the engagements with Messrs. Johnstone and Stuart, who agreed with me that it would be paid me wherever and whenever I wished to establish myself in a land not under the dominion of the King of England. That is easy to verify by the representation that I will make of the demands which I have made, which were agreed to in their entirety by Messrs. Johnstone and Stuart.

Collated copy of the letter written by M. the Chevalier Montault de Monberaut, Deputy Superintendent in the Province of West Florida.

To M. Aubry, Commandant of French troops, and, for the interim, of the Province of Louisiana.

Mobile, 7th March 1765

SIR:

I am come to pass some days at my estate. On my arrival here I was apprised of the death of Monsieur d'Abbadie. I sincerely felicitate you upon the happy circumstance which furnishes you the occasion to bring your great talents to light, and the sentiments of integrity and probity which you profess. I wish you a long continuation of prosperity, and above all that some turn of iniquity does not arrest the wheel of fortune which proves to turn so happily for you.

I will act, with regard to you, Sir, with more respect than I did with M. d'Abbadie. I avow that I owed it to his position, but his person interdicted me from all acts of attention and consideration.

I will therefore, myself, give you my own side of the course I took on entering into the service of the English in the capacity of Deputy Superintendent for all the affairs relative to the Indians in the Province of West Florida.

I am not unaware that my proceeding has found plenty of critics in New Orleans. Perhaps my greatest detractors would like to be in my place; or at least, if they were instructed in all of my reasons, if they would not approve of me, I am persuaded that they would rest in balance between approbation and blame.

Be that as it may, Sir, the thing is done. I am persuaded that you know me sufficiently to be convinced that I shall serve the King of England with the same zeal, the same fidelity, and the same feelings of honor and probity which I have always professed and given evidence of when I had the honor of serving the King of France.

I hope, Sir, that seeing the good union which reigns between the crowns of France and England, you will accord me your good offices in order to put me in a position to execute and lead to a happy end the operations with which I shall be charged. You can be assured that on my side, as long as that good union may last, I will eagerly welcome the occasions which will present themselves, with regard to the employment that I have, in order to aid, facilitate, and procure every sort of surety to the French and to the Spanish when they shall have taken possession of the land which His Most Christian Majesty has ceded them. I ardently desire that the good intelligence between the crowns may be of long duration, and that between us we can, for a long time, carry on a contest of good manners and lend our mutual aid. It is with such sentiments that I have the honor of being, with the utmost esteem,

Sir,

Your most humble and
Most obedient servant

Signed: Le Cher De Montaut de Monberaut

Below is written

We, knight of the royal and military order of St. Louis, Commandant for the King in Louisiana,

Certify to all those whom it may concern, that this letter is exact and conforms to the letter that the Chevalier de Montaut de Monberaut wrote me from Mobile on the date of the seventh March 1765. *Signed:* Aubry

Copy of the first letter which Mr. Johnstone, Governor of West Florida, wrote on arriving in this land.

To M. le Chevalier de Montault de Monberaut
from Pensacola, the *1st* November *1764*

SIR:

I am informed on all sides that you are a man of merit, intelligence, and of great ascendancy among the Alabamas. I wish very strongly to be able to reconcile the temper of these people to the British government. Consequently, I would esteem myself happy if, by my candid and sincere conduct, I could gain your friendship and theirs. Hobbes says that riches are power, and I, that power must in many cases command riches. I wish to be able to discourse with you on that subject, quite content to accord to each the ascendancy that it ought to have in society, and avowing openly that Indian policy is a very important object for the government of this Province.

I have believed that it is better to make this declaration in a few words than to try to gain my point by long detours which would only serve to deceive you.

I have the honor of being,

Sir,

Your most humble and most
obedient servant

Signed: Geo. Johnstone.

Copy of the letter of invitation to M. le Chevalier de Montault de Monberaut, written by Messrs. Johnstone and Stuart, the first Governor of the Province of West Florida, and the other Superintendent of Indian Affairs in the southern part of America.

SIR:

After having admired the *combat* of passion and honor on the subject of religion and the love of your native land that you have so well expressed in the conversations that we have had with you, we have maturely examined those two objects and have clearly seen that principally your religion was an invincible obstacle for you to be able to take the employment which your birth and merit would require us to solicit for you on the part of His Britannic Majesty.

But as we very well know the profound knowledge that you have in Indian politics and as we cannot ignore the happy successes that have crowned the negotiations with which you have been charged in regard to those Nations, we clearly see that the good of the King's service demands that we invite you, in the name of his said Majesty, to give us your opinion and your aid in bringing the Indian Nations to the point of concluding with the English nation a sound and lasting peace.

We ask nothing of you, Sir, contrary to the sentiments of honor which you profess.

When His Most Christian Majesty ceded to His Britannic Majesty Mobile, as well as a portion of those possessions on the Mississippi, he surely did not intend to keep any of his subjects from indicating and facilitating to the English the means of taking tranquil possession.

We come now, in a short and clear manner, which is always the most correct way to work, to place before you the offers which we can make in the name and for the service of His Britannic Majesty, recognizing at the same time that your great merit can command much more if your conscience will permit you to conform to the terms which the laws of England order in such occasions.

Primarily we desire you to take an oath to serve His Majesty faithfully during all the time that you will be employed in his service. By means of this oath we shall make you commissioner of Indian affairs in this Province; consequently we will give you a commission which will be valid until His Majesty has made his intentions known thereupon.

As soon as that commission is received, you must do your utmost to bring to Mobile or Pensacola the chief whom we call The Mortar, and whom you call the war chief Le Loup, and whom you will try to attach to the interest of the English nation.

To accomplish this end, you will be permitted to spend up to the sum of one hundred pounds sterling for gifts which you may judge suitable to give him. You will obey all orders that you may receive from the one or the other of us relative to the savages' affairs. We engage ourselves, in recompense for these services, to pay you the sum of two hundred ten pounds sterling a year, of which we will pay to you one hundred pounds sterling the same day that you accept our offer. We obligate ourselves further to furnish you a house, or pay you fifty pounds for renting one to your taste. The titles of the land which you have owned will be confirmed. You will furnish provisions for all the savages of all ranks below the first.

You will also be reimbursed for all extraordinary expenses, and we promise to recommend you to His Majesty's ministers for a pension more ample than that which we are authorized to give you, and also to recommend your children.

And in general you can count on being treated with that civility and respect which your distinguished merit ought to command everywhere.

We are with profound respect,

Sir,

Your most humble servants

Mobile, 8th Decr 1764 *Signed*

Geo Johnstone

and John Stuart

Below is written

To Monsieur le Chevalier de Montaut de Monberaut

Copy of the reply which the Chevalier de Montault de Monberaut made to the preceding letter

Mobile, 13th December, 1764.

GENTLEMEN:

It is very gratifying to me to have been able to excite your admiration by my manner of expressing myself on the subject of the religion which I profess and my love for my native land, so I will not enter into greater detail on those points, having already explained myself clearly enough to you directly in the private conversations which we have had together.

You do me the honor, gentlemen, of inviting me, in the name of His Britannic Majesty, to make use of the knowledge that I have in Indian politics and essaying whether the ascendancy which I formerly had over the minds of these Nations can determine them to contract a firm and lasting alliance with the English, alleging, in order to persuade me, that you demand nothing contrary to my honor, inasmuch as His Most Christian Majesty, in ceding Mobile &c. to His Britannic Majesty has not intended to prohibit any of his former or present subjects facilitating to the English the means of taking peaceable possession, &c.

I am too well persuaded, gentlemen, of the esteem which you give evidence of having for me, not to be convinced that you do not wish to engage me in measures contrary to the sentiments of honor with which I have always been filled; and I think, even as you, that the King of France will never find it wrong that one of his subjects facilitated the English in the means of taking peaceable possession of the land that he has ceded. And it is in this persuasion that I will accept the invitation you extend to me if the following conditions are agreeable.

Before speaking of the advantages which you offer me, I am going to have the honor, gentlemen, of responding to the conditions which you set forth. I will receive from you the commission which you offer provisional to that which you propose to ask for me from His Majesty.

I will take the oath, which you require, to serve His Britannic Majesty faithfully during the whole time I may be employed in his service; but my oath will be only for the term of said service and not in the capacity of a subject, my final decision on the place where I am going to fix my residence not yet having been made. And I hope that in recognition of my services, if I decide to remain an English subject, I shall have the same rights that His Majesty has accorded to the former inhabitants of the lands ceded to England who have, in the time limit of the treaty, declared themselves of their free will subjects of England and have taken the oath of loyalty and obedience. And if my affairs or my inclination prompt me to go to live in some land subject to another rule, I ask that I be given every facility for moving myself, my family and effects, as well as for giving me, or the purchasers whom I may find, time to complete the sale of my property. And I ask that until I have made my decision, I may be able to sell, buy property, peaceably enjoy that which I have if the purchasers judge proper to cancel their bargains—in a word, that I may enjoy the same advantages that those enjoy who are sworn subjects of England.

I ask the same advantages for a family which is attached to my interests. I have already had the honor of speaking to you about them.

I shall obey the orders which you give me, whether the said orders are addressed to me signed by both together or by one of you alone. I hope, gentlemen, if that which you order me to do does not coincide with my ideas, you will permit me to present the objections which I shall think consonant with the good of the service, it being well understood at all times that, if the thing should demand prompt execution, I will conform exactly to the orders that I will have received.

I ask also, gentlemen, not to be subjected to receiving orders nor rendering accounts except to you two or persons occupying your places if it please His Majesty to employ you otherwise. I mean by this article, gentlemen, that I ask not to be subjected to rendering accounts to persons invested with rank inferior to yours; but if the good of the service requires that I send some memorial or render some account to the English ministry, or to the Board of Trade, and to the general commanding the troops in America, not only will I obey their orders with pleasure, but it will be a real honor to enter into correspondence with their lordships.

I will do my utmost and concert with integrity with you, gentlemen, for means of making The Mortar and all the outstanding chiefs in the Nations come to Mobile and attach themselves to the interest of the English nation. As to the expenditure which you authorize me to make for that object and for gifts, I find it truly considerable, but nevertheless it might well be insufficient; however, gentlemen, as you will be on the spot, you will take charge of everything, and I will not enter into that affair except to give my advice.

I pass next, gentlemen, to the proposals you make of fixing my salary at the sum of two hundred ten pounds sterling, fifty pounds sterling to rent a house, &c. As these appointments are not nearly sufficient to compensate me for the expenses that I will be obliged to make in that regard, as I have shown by the particular reasons which you will find in detail below, I beg you, gentlemen, to permit me not to accept any other conclusion of terms than that which His Majesty or his ministry shall decide. I shall only ask you, as I am short of ready money for establishing a household in town, that you will advance to me the sum of two hundred pounds sterling from the treasury, for which I will give my note and be my own surety in my own name for repayment.

I put it thus, gentlemen, to prove that the honor of being useful to the human race and to the King, the father of an illustrious nation, holds the place of principal compensation, relying for the rest on all that it will please him to decide in my favor.

As to lodging, I have retained today that which Major Farmar presently occupies. I have agreed to pay him, with the land which is adjoining, the sum of seven hundred *piastres gourdes.* You will decide what you wish to allow me for a lodging; I will pay the balance.

I also ask you, gentlemen, to fix a sum for the salary of a secretary, if you do not prefer that it be an article of extraordinary expense. As I do not know English, someone to interpret items relative to the good of the service will be invaluable.

I take those measures which you solicit from me, gentlemen, toward procuring the tranquility of the three white nations which inhabit this continent, to wit: the English, the French and the Spanish. In view of the union which reigns among them, their interests are the same. Since my object should be to render it advantageous to all, and as it is not doubtful that it will be, if we succeed it could be interpreted to my disadvantage, which would undoubtedly do me harm. As I believe it just that in some fashion indemnities equal sacrifices, I ask, if I am put out of work, to be treated as true Englishmen are—that is to say, that I will be paid an annual pension of one half of my salary wherever I may settle, or that an equivalent lump-sum gratification will be credited to me in one payment.

Concerning the offer you make, gentlemen, of confirming the titles of land which I have owned, I shall have the honor of presenting the said titles to you, and as the said lands are sold, if the purchasers wish to keep them for themselves, I have explained my demands to you, which I hope will be granted.

The promise you make, gentlemen, of recommending me and my children to His Majesty's ministry is extremely advantageous to me; I hope, if we have the good fortune to bring the negotiations we are about to enter in concert to a happy end, I hope, I say, that if we have the good fortune to succeed, you will have the kindness to dispatch my elder son to carry the news to His Majesty and to his ministry, in fine, to all those to whom it ought to be carried. My said son will come in for his part in our operations, for I am going to send him to feel out The Mortar and the other chiefs to whom he is known.

My son and I, gentlemen, have complete confidence in your good offices. We know no one in England; only our good services can procure us favor. It will be under your eyes, gentlemen, that I shall execute all my operations; therefore you cannot be deceived in the accounts that you will have to render about the zeal that I will employ to procure for you the conclusion of the treaty which you consider making with the Indians. To be sure, I will not undertake to provide an absolute guarantee, but I think I can win your praise.

I believe it also necessary, gentlemen, to warn you that the Indians have been accustomed by the French to very affectionate treatment; their chiefs, every time they would come in to a settlement, were first entertained, as were their warriors; there was always something for them to eat at the interpreter's house. Further, they never failed to appear at mealtime at the house of the person in charge of their affairs, who was the commandant of the place. The Medal Chiefs and some of the more important ones ate at the commandant's table; the commissioned captains ate apart, in a place somewhat distinguished from their warriors, but all ate some dishes from the commandant's table, who for that reason prepared repasts at the king's expense. When the chiefs returned, they ordinarily received some little gift and some subsistence for their trip. These visits were repeated often during the course of the year.

Since you show confidence in me, gentlemen, I am obliged to say that I believe that it is indispensable to conform yourselves in everything to the customs of the French, particularly for a few years. It would be very dangerous to reform by yourselves.* I know them all, having had the honor for several years of having the direction of the important tribes. You may be assured that I will economize to the best of my ability in order not to put the state to useless expense. I say this to you, asking you to consider that this

* I see, gentlemen, that you are surprised that some savages are punctual at dinner time. I warn you that it will be worse at the time of the congress, when the Indians will be here. You cannot take a step, especially when mealtime approaches, without having four or five hundred following you about.

colony is new-born; not being established anywhere, you therefore need a solid peace in order to save the blood of your new settlers, and if the Indians find some difference in the new government to their disadvantage, the poor colonists would be very exposed.

I pass next, gentlemen, into the details of the expenses to which I am obligated by the commission which you would give me. First, from the day on which I shall be declared responsible for the affairs of the savages, it will be necessary that I fix my residence in town. Consequently, I will be obliged to place a steward over my plantation, whose wages, subsistence and other expenses will amount to more than fifty pounds sterling. You are not unaware, gentlemen, of the proverb invented by Æsop which says that the eye of the master fattens the horse; he might well have said also, the land; so I do not hope that my steward will procure for me the same revenue that I would be able to make for myself.

Secondly, when I am at my estate I lead a regulated and inexpensive life. My herdsmen, while watching my herds, occupy themselves in hunting and ordinarily bring me enough game of all sorts to maintain a table that would pass for sumptuous in town. Of this, all who do me the honor of coming to visit me can give you an account. In fixing my residence in town, I am deprived of that advantage; experience proves to you that life is very costly in Mobile.

Thirdly, in the country I can go about simply dressed; living in town, although not given to sumptuousness, that expense is more than three or four times greater, especially because of having to treat daily with the Indians who respect a person according only to the brilliance of his dress.

Fourthly, resident upon my estate, I need only one or two domestics who ordinarily find several hours in the day for working in the garden or other useful labor; residing in town, I would no longer have the same comfort, but rather I would need to augment the number of my domestics. If I take them from the number of negroes that I have already, that will be fewer hands on my place, resulting in the diminution of revenue.

Fifthly, houses which are for rent in Mobile are ordinarily without any sort of furniture. I will consequently be obliged to make an extraordinary expenditure in order to render habitable that which I have rented. I will not enter into a longer detail of expenses indispensable to a commissioner appointed for Indian affairs.

I have set before you, gentlemen, the most considerable and inevitable expenses in order to show you that the sums you are authorized to fix for my appointments are scarcely sufficient to indemnify me for half the losses and expenses that I will be obliged to make, without any mention of compensation for the trouble I would give myself—which will be great. Therefore, I hope you will have the kindness, gentlemen, to advise His Majesty's ministry and the Board of Trade so that they will see that I do not seek to make His Majesty pay for my services above their value. I believe them too just to require that in expatriating myself I spend the little substance forming the patrimony of my children in order to fulfill the honors of my employment. The treatment which is given me can alone determine me to the complete sacrifice of my residence.

If my conduct is badly interpreted, I stand to lose, on the French side, first, the Croix de St. Louis, which was awarded to me in 1759, and pensions which my son and I have earned by our services. I can still have some hope of sharing in the family property, which becomes void on declaring myself subject to another crown.

I have indicated, gentlemen, what hopes I can form of being received into the service of Spain with the rank of colonel; these hopes, in truth, may only come to nought; perhaps, however, they may have their effect.

One particular concern of mine is that I own half of a plantation, situated one and a half leagues from New Orleans, on which there are a planing mill, some negroes, and cattle. If the Spanish or the French disapprove of my accepting a commission from the English, not only will I have no more hope of having employment with them, but perhaps I will even lose my property; in this case, I will have recourse to the justice and protection of His Britannic Majesty for the recovery of my property or my indemnification.

I have thought it necessary, gentlemen, to set forth these details to prove to you that the sacrifices I make are sure guarantees of the zeal with which I have planned to serve.

I have the honor of being, with profound respect
Gentlemen
Your most humble and most
obedient servant

Signed Monberaut.

Copy of the reply of Messrs. Johnstone and Stuart to the preceding letter.

SIR

We have received your letter in answer to that which we had the honour to write to you. We agree entirely to the terms. The two hundred pounds shall be paid immediately; if we succeed in the treaty, your son shall be sent to England; but that everything that depends on us may be fixed, we now mark one hundred pounds p. annum to be allowed you for the rent of your house.

The charge of Clerk will come under that of Extraordinaries.
We are with great respect
Sir
Your most obedt &
most humble Ser[t]

Signed Geo Johnstone
and John Stuart

Copy of the Chevalier de Montault de Monberaut's letter to Messrs. Johnstone and Stuart which Mr. Johnstone says is a long, vain, tedious, and puffing memorial.

Mobile, 20 June 1765

GENTLEMEN:

My son, on returning from Pensacola, stopped at Forneret's; that fellow informed him that Mr. McGillivray had told him, as something of which he was quite certain, that M. de Monberaut was going to be released from his employment.

The instructions which Mr. Stuart gave me at the time of my departure from Pensacola are proof, gentlemen, that that man's gossip stems from malice for which I demand that he be punished.

While I believe that the course McGillivray has held is solely a product of his imagination, I cannot hide from you, gentlemen, that it has been preceded by the greatest coldness between us—which causes me to reflect and, thereupon, to hope that you will not find what I have done for you to have been bad.

A long time before you sought me out, in order to make use of the confidence which the savages have in me so as to bring the operations with which you were charged to a happy end, His Excellency General Gage himself invited me to take employment in the service of His Britannic Majesty. I communicated to you the letters which the general did me the honor of writing, letters which are full of signs of his esteem for me. I did not leave you ignorant of the fact that, not wishing to live the life of a mere private individual, I sought to procure myself a situation, and in the circumstances of the country I was put in the position of entering the service of the first of the three crowns of France, Spain or England that would give me employment agreeable to my feelings.

I have communicated my opinions to you on the measures which were taken to woo me to the employment of either France or Spain.

After mature examination and reiterated entreaties, you finally made up your minds to make me written propositions, to which I made my observations and established the conditions on which I would accept the employment which you proposed to me. My conditions having been accepted without any reservations on your part, I received from you the commission for the position I now occupy, which you have assured me was a permanent position.

Scarcely had I begun my duties than the jealous laid their batteries for my ruin. I have been aware of that for a long time.

Your choice was, however, fully justified, gentlemen, and the results have entirely corresponded with the opinion which you indicated you had of me. The Choctaws, among whom I have less credit than among the Tallapoosas, Cowetas, and Abihkas, have not left you ignorant of the satisfaction which they had in seeing me employed in their affairs, and you cannot doubt that it was my exhortation which determined the chiefs of the Eastern Division to sacrifice to the English the medals and commissions which they had received from the French.

The Mortar and the other Creek chiefs who came to parley at the Congress of Pensacola have not ceased repeating that, rejecting all the invitations that had been made from every side, they gave in only to mine, which they would perhaps even then have spurned had it not been buttressed by the embassy which I sent them through my son.

I have, with Colonel Wedderburn, gone to confront that haughty nation which I have led to you in the posture of suppliants; and in the petty difficulties which arose in the Congress on the subject of land, as on the subject of the reduction of trade prices which they demanded, it has been demonstrated that they gave in easily only to the representations and exhortations which I made to them.

I have not mentioned, Sir, the signs of especial friendship which the chiefs and leading men of the Choctaw and Creek Nations have given me. Let it suffice to say that, conforming to the sentiments of right and honor which I have always professed, I have done everything for the good of the English nation.

At the time when you sought me out, gentlemen, the forces of His Britannic Majesty had not had the same success which they have had since. Now all the Nations which made war on the English are subjugated and have been constrained to implore the clemency of the conqueror.*

Circumstances being changed, my services are perhaps not as necessary as they appeared to be at the time when you sought me out. Perhaps this would have given cause for the language which Mr. McGillivray has used, but as I have fulfilled my commission with honor and rectitude, and as successes have even surpassed the expectations which I gave you, I am within my rights in demanding that the conditions which were made with me be

* This has been put in the exposé of the governor and the superintendent which is false, for there are still some Nations which are in arms against the English.

executed. Therefore, gentlemen, if in this state of affairs, my character as a foreigner and a Catholic renders my services incompatible with the constitution of the state, I would hold you truly obligated 1. To give me fair notice. 2. To fulfill accordingly the promises which you have made me, which consist on your part of confirming the titles of land which I possessed, giving me titles of ownership for purchases which I have made since the agreement which we made together. 3. To secure for me from the ministry a patent for a pension, payable in whatever place I may establish myself, of half my appointments (which are less than those you offered), or if it is more advantageous for the state to give me a gift in lieu of the pension, it ought to be at least 1,050 pounds sterling, which is the amount of the life annuity of 105 pounds sterling, which should come up to the annual pension which would be due me when I am released from employment. 4. I hope, gentlemen, that if you take away my employment, sufficient time will be given me to make my decision on the course that I wish to take, and that up to the moment at which I make that decision I may enjoy the privileges which the king accords his declared subjects. 5. That if I determine to go to take up residence in some territory which is not under English dominion, that all the time necessary to me will be given me to sell my possessions, and that all facilities for transportation will be furnished for myself, my effects, &c., for me to return to the place where I wish to fix my residence.

The conditions stipulated above, gentlemen, are those to which you have subscribed and which, in that case, I can repeat as something due to me.

As I really cannot doubt that those who envy me are capable of anything, I ask you, gentlemen, to be so good as to give me a reply on which I can form a plan for the conduct of my affairs.

As I think that it will be necessary for a final decision, about that which concerns me, to have that of the ministry or of the Lords Commissioners of Trade, I warn you, gentlemen, that it will be only after the arrival of their Lordship's reply that I can determine whether I shall remain subject to the King of England or not. While awaiting the court's decision, I shall remain as I am, faithful to the oath I have taken between your hands, of serving His Majesty faithfully, with zeal, &c., as long as I may be employed in the capacity of deputy superintendent, &c.

On arrival here, gentlemen, I have received news of my property and law suits in New Orleans. There are even some who say that I run the risk that it will be confiscated to the profit of the King of France or of Spain. I am going to send my elder son to inform me of the true state of those affairs, and pursuant to the reply which I shall receive from him, I shall ask your permission to go to New Orleans myself to make plans for avoiding the danger of losing it. But if, in spite of all my precautions, I am so unfortunate that, because of my position as servant of the King of England, I should suffer confiscation, I hope that the conditions which I have stipulated on this subject will be executed.

I have the honor of being, with respect,

Your most humble and most obedient servant

Signed Le Chevalier de Montault de Monberaut

[Mobile 20 June 1765]

[In the manuscript of the "Mémoire Justificatif," the following letter from Gov. George Johnstone to Monberaut is translated into French. Although essentially accurate, the translated version inevitably loses something of the acidity of Johnstone's original communication which is reprinted here in order to display exactly those insults which so directly touched the Frenchman's honor. Subsequent fragmentary quotations from this letter, used by Monberaut as points of reference for his justification, derive from his translation and will be found to vary from the original. That differentiation has been retained for further illustration of the degree of misunderstanding which characterized the two men's relations from beginning to end.]

Pensacola, 26 June 1765

SIR

I should not deign to send any answer to the long, vain, tedious puffing Memorial which you have addressed to Mr. Stuart and me, as I am certain you must be conscious of the weakness of every part of it, if I did not see it was calculated for more distant ends by laying a basis for a second means how to deceive others and vindicate the extraordinary conduct you have held in past & the more wicked you are about to perpetrate.

This behaviour puts me in mind of what Swift relates of the Yahoos when they are seized in any acts of fraud and forgiven, as soon as they get at a little distance, they mount the first tree & begin to bespatter their benefactor, and to dignify their own importance; and so rooted is evil in them, says this author, that in case you was dispos'd to pardon them a thousand times they wou'd still repeat the same acts of ingratitude.

You seem to make a prodigious charge of your own time and to think very little of mine; if we are to judge by the length and number of the representations concerning the Count de Montberraut & the Chevalier de Montaut De Monberaut and at length plain Mons. de Montbereaut all of which are not three persons, but one good Catholick who offer'd himself as a mediator, and sacrific'd all that he had for the sake of the poor naked Indians, nay even immolated his Bullocks & sold his wig & washed his brows in vinegar & gall & purged his body to clear his brain to serve them.

From the state of the representation it is confessed that so strange a memorial did not proceed from what McGillivray said to Ferneret, and Ferneret said to your son & your son said to you, but from the *froidure* which Mr. Stuart & I had shewn you some time before.

This *froidure,* then, was known when we parted; it could not have been since. The explanation should have been at that time, but you well knew it was impossible to support the allegations of the memorial face to face, and you was also sensible Mr. Stuart was sailed, otherwise you would not have wrote such a paper, and so you imagined you would throw me into some embarrass[ment] until we could hear from him, and in the mean time any double intrigue you might pursue might be palliated.

I would rather at any time have the whole family of the Montbereauts, great, numerous & powerfull as they are, with the three Crowns of England, France & Spain & also with the Chactaws, Abekas, Cowetas, & Tallipousses, my open enemies, than one of them my false friend.

You will find I do not want resolution to determine when pushed to a point, tho' I thought it would have been much better as I told

Mr. Stuart to have waited the decision of the Ministry in England on your subject, ill as your behaviour has been. However, as nothing can satisfy your restless disposition, and that I can easily conceive the disappointment which your unsatiable avarice hath met in being tied up to so strict an œconomy, I shall now propose two things for your consideration— The first is, to come and reside at Pensacola till your affairs in West Florida can be finished, & to embark in three days from the receipt of this letter. The other is, to embark in four days for New Orleans. Otherwise I have issued a warrant to take you into custody as a man suspected of carrying on schemes destructive to the government and your process shall be regularly made.

However as you tell me you want to depart for New Orleans to settle the very weighty affairs you have in [that] colony, and as I wish to do every thing with the greatest moderation consistent with the safety of the colony, I think a journey there would be the most agreeable. In the meanwhile I suspend you from all the cares of the Indians, which have so much oppressed you for the seven days you have had the charge, or any transaction with them of any kind whatsoever, even to the buying & retailing of venison thro' a second, third or fourth hand. Now that our business is finished I will answer your Memorial article by article.

Art. 1 Your son is a boy very much spoiled by the natural disposition of his mind, by the haughty puffs and low intrigues of his acquaintance. The Sieur Ferneret was a soldier, writes a good hand, spells better than any of the French, married a pretty woman by a pretty puff his mind is allways on the fret. Mr. McGillivray has been much among the Creoles of Guadaloupe, he is at present sick & delerious, tho' on this occasion he may pass for a prophet.

[*Art.*] 2 If Mr. Stuart's instructions were a sufficient proof that Mr. McGillivray's report was false, it should have satisfied you, and not have been marked as the ground of so extraordinary a memorial. Perhaps McGillivray asserted as the almanack makers were wont, after that Louis the Fourteenth was afflicted with a *fistulo in ano* to predict his death in every edition, so probably McGillivray in settling your accounts, found a latent disease that must in time destroy you, and perhaps you said unto yourself, as that mighty monarch said unto his friends, "Those Dogs must surely be right at last and therefore I ought to prepare for the worst."

[*Art.*] 3 That much coolness on our part did precede this relation of McGillivray's is certain.

From the time that we first came to treat with you we acquainted you with the publick œconomy which prevailed in our government, more particularly at this time when a real honest man is placed at the head of the finances after a very expensive & burthensome war. We told you how strictly our hands were tied up and the risk we ran in our own private fortunes by the stretches we had made. That we saw the necessity of some greater expense than we were allowed in treating with nations whose situation was not perfectly understood by the ministry when they settled the plan of expense relative to them, yet nevertheless, every such expense was to be managed with the utmost frugality & that we expected you would concur in every measure of that kind. Whereas on the contrary, we found that as soon as you had got the slightest power, notwithstanding the pain you observed it gave us, you was endeavouring by every means, direct & indirect to accumulate charges, & to render the minds of the Indians discontent with their presents. Puffing away what the French used to give; maintaining the spirit of party amongst the Chiefs, and carrying on intrigues with the interpreters, & other persons, to attest your accounts, very much below the character in which you stood. This easily convinced us that a real conscientious discharge of the office you had accepted was not your view, but on the contrary, a selfish transitory profit was looked for.

There needs no greater proof of this than your account with Mr. Stuart. Vinegar, pepper & salt, eight dollars a day, in a country abounding with sour wine & salt provisions, is not the most astonishing article. I know nothing like it except an innkeeper, at Canterbury, who being informed that the person who had taken up his quarters at his house was the French Ambassador he immediately declared he should pay for all the damage he had lost in custom during the war, and accordingly he charged the Ambassador about eight dollars a dish & a guinea a bottle for wine; which with the sumptuous manner those gentlemen are accustomed to live in, amounted, *quelques choses* and all, to about three hundred pounds sterling. I believe it can be proved if this matter comes to be tried that the publick bread was sold by your own family thro' the streets of Mobile.

Art. 4 & 5 A long time before we sought you to make use of the confidence that the savages had in you to bring to a happy issue the operations with which we were charged, you had entered into negotiations with Col. Robinson [i.e., Robertson] who had engaged Gen. Gage to correspond with you on that subject. Your demands had been so extravagant that the negotiation had been broke off. Certainly the general's letters were full of politeness, but how he could have so particular an esteem for you as you intimate, without knowing you, I cannot so easily conceive. His esteem could only be founded on the esteem which you could render his country, & the continuation of it can be no longer than you have discharged your trust with good faith. You did shew us a parcel of papers, all calculated to promote your own consequence. How a maid, to a maid of honor that was no maid, was to get you the rank of Colonel in Spain, how a secretary to an under secretary who was no secretary was to get you a Croix de St. Louis in France, and also a long branch of your descent from Adam. I told you then as I tell you now, that a man could not have lived three weeks in the world not to have seen thro' all that froth which had nothing to do with our negotiation. That your speaking Choctaw, and having lived at Alibamont were greater recommendations to me than any of those papers which had all the appearance of being wrote on the occasion.

Art. 6 After a thorough examination and several discourses which would have been very long if we had not endeavoured to drive away the scum, we did agree, at your request, to make the proposition in writing which was not very long, I am sure, on our part, but to which you returned observations concerning your family, your cook, your œconome, your batterie de cuisine and your cloaths, all so different from what had passed that I really considered you as a man overpowered with vanity and told you plainly I would have no more to say to you, at which you seemed very much struck and offered to cut off all the superfluous matter. Upon this a new proposition was entered into. You begged we would alter the letter which was first sent and that you would draw such a letter as would vindicate your conduct the better with the French & Spaniards, in case your religion was found incompatible with the employment you was to accept of. I told you it was indifferent to me what cream of compliment you chose to bestow on yourself, that I would subscribe to it provided the substance was the same. That in all matters of business with men of sense, instead of adding, it allways weakened the merit of the party. Matters being thus adjusted, like address and answer, the whole was finished as it now stands. However plain I am now in my expression, you are conscious I was not less so at the time of settling this point.

Art. 7 I am sorry you had so many enemies then, have so many now, and are likely to have so many for the time to come unless God shall work a change that is not likely to happen at your time of life.

Art. 8 Our choice is so far vindicated that you had the power of doing great good. We have endeavoured to prevent you from doing much mischief; that you was disposed to do a great deal, we could not have foretold till we tried.

Art. 9 We found that among the Choctaws you had no credit but what our power gave you. You endeavoured to raise a credit by keeping up a distinction of party & by the means of a very scandalous interpreter you abused the confidence we had put in you & made speeches for some of them to pronounce which we traced to their source as soon as delivered. These things I know of my own knowledge. With respect to the party of the East I was not present, but Mr. Stuart told me, who I believe as honest and sincere a man as exists in the universe, that you had endeavoured to pervert their minds, and to make a mountain of a mole hill, as was generally the case & that it was only owing to his determined manner of acting, and throwing off all the frivolous matter which was brought to involve the simplest action in the greatest mystery that he succeeded.

Art. 10 I must acquaint you that I am not insensible how far the same kind of intrigue was endeavoured to be played on the Mortar, & how far your son was directed to write the very vain letters which he did from that Nation, but he is only a boy and ought to obey his father.

I do acknowledge you had great merit in knowing so surely where Topulga lay, who was the instrument employed by you, in bringing down the Mortar. But you must as candidly confess that our presents had some effect in operating on his conduct.

The Mortar himself declared publickly that it was chiefly on the persuasion of Mr. Struthers that he came down, & that you had more than once asked him thro' Topulga, to declare it was owing to you which he never would do. I never can think the obligation of sending your son so great as you seem to state it—tho' I shall not endeavour to lessen the further reward I have recommended to Government. Your son was well fed, well guarded, & better paid than his father used to be for the Commission which he bore in the French service. I dare say it's more money than he ever earned in his life or is likely to earn for three years to come, besides the different gratifications he was permitted to distribute.

Art. 11 You did press your service to go out and meet the Creeks and Col. Wedderburne was generous enough to accompany you. I told you, before your departure, I thought your harangue was entirely improper, & I was not sorry to hear, those natural people would not hear above the first sentence. As to the farce which was acted by that haughty Nation, & the humiliating posture you describe, you certainly have the merit of it.

It is true, I am a witness, they always yielded to your representations, because you was both the author and the queller of them, always ready to deliver the mountain of a mouse & to magnify a mouse into a mountain. This I can fairly say, that I never knew any mischief during the Congress that was not brooded in my anti-chamber.*

Art. 12 Living upon the land belonging to the King of Great

* N. B. Monsr. Montberaut was sick & lodged in the Governor's house.

Britain, it was your duty from the first of cession to have done every thing in your power to reconcile the minds of the Indians to his Majesty's Government. How far your authority with the Chiefs will prevail, when situated in another country, destitute of our presents, we shall experience even after the influence which we have added to it.

For my part I say with Ajax, "Good Gods! let me but engage in the open daylight."

Art. 13 The Alteration of circumstances will never make any alteration in our own conduct in fulfilling, with honesty & fidelity the engagements we have entered into which always supposes a reciprocal integrity.

Art. 14 Your character being now thoroughly known, it is certain there are few persons who are acquainted with it who would think your services necessary, or who would chuse to employ you if they could avoid it. Nevertheless I could have wished it had been possible to have acted with you till we could have heard from England, because there is a decency in separating I should have been glad to have preserved. If you have discharged your commission with honor & exactness, you certainly have a right to the stipulations. Neither under all the subtleties which have been practiced are we wishing to deprive you of the advantages. National honor will be better preserved by disdaining the dirty wages.

You seem to mention the circumstances of your being a Catholic rendering you incapable of any employment by the Constitution of England as a new matter which had just been communicated to you, whereas you know it was mentioned over & over, it was likewise communicated to you in the letter from Gen. Gage. Tho' we are not certain how far it is in the power of the administration to evite the general rule.

With respect to the Articles of Capitulation they cannot be stronger if I was to sign them a thousand times here, than they are by the first agreement, tho' I do deny that they are in any measure correspondent to those which you have stated.

I think you have acted nine days, & you demand an annual pension greater than the full pay you had from the King of France, but these matters by the agreement are left to the determination of the Ministry. But it is only for a course of long, extraordinary and faithful services such rewards are granted.

You shall have all the time which common justice can ask to remain in the province to prepare matters for your departure, but I hope you will not take it amiss that I do insist, your residence shall be at Pensacola while you are settling your affairs. As you have not proved a worthy servant to the King, you cannot expect the privileges which he only grants to such. Those who are determined to follow your fortune must leave the Province in one month from the delivery of this letter, or take the oath of allegiance to his Majesty, excepting your own children & two white servants, also any one person you may chuse to leave here to take care of your affairs, who must take the oath of fidelity to the King during four months he is allowed to stay here on that business.

Art. 15 As I can no longer doubt of all the information which has been given me, after seeing this memorial under your own hand, I have sent the answer, from which you may form a plan to regulate your affairs.

Art. 16 I did think it would have been necessary to have waited the decision of the Ministry on the matters which concern you, but as the preceding part of your letter carries quite a different import, and as it is impossible such weighty matters can be entrusted in such slippery hands, on whose fidelity we can have no dependence, and as the power on such occasions is left with me, I have therefore exercised [it] in the manner the most beneficial to His Majesty's service, willing to preserve public engagements pure and inviolable, willing to shew every act of humility to individuals, but determined that the safety of the Province shall be the first object of my care.

[*Art. 17*] As you have received advice from New Orleans, that your goods there are prosecuted, the sooner you go there the better. I hope there is as little foundation in this report as there [is] in that of the letter you shewed me wherein it's marked that Mr. Aubry had detained your Croix de St. Louis. If the King of England is to pay for your effects, I make no doubt, both that they will be condemned, and amount to a pretty large sum.

I have had some little trouble in saving your son from a very vexatious prosecution, that of horse stealing, but as I supposed he imagined himself still in the Indian Nation, he had not that turpitude of mind which the law supposes to accompany such an action.

I have nothing further to add than to assure you these are my final resolutions on your subject, & therefore you will not expect I will again employ any more time in answering any more memorials which may be sent.

I am— Sir
Your most obedient and
most humble Servant
Signed/ George Johnstone

Copied from an exact copy
taken from the original
by Gov. Johnstone's Secretary
by me
Ch: Stuart

The Mémoire Justificatif

Of the Chevalier de Montault de Monberaut in his capacity as Deputy Superintendent for Indian Affairs in the Province of West Florida, the said Mémoire serving as refutation and answer to the false and calumnious charges made against him by Mr. George Johnstone, Governor of the said Province of West Florida.

Memorial to be Presented to the King of England

What could be more ridiculous than the letter written to me by Governor Johnstone, dated June 27, 1765. Unlike him, I shall not say that I do not owe it to him to reply. His position as Governor of the Province puts me under the dire necessity of making it known to the public that his aforesaid letter is no less full of impostures and calumnies than of expressions deprived of good sense.

He says "that he has seen that my memorial was calculated for more distant ends by laying a basis for a second means how to deceive others and justifying the extraordinary conduct I have held in the past and the more wicked I am about to perpetrate."

In spite of the obscurity which such nonsense casts, one sees that his lunatic frenzy* has not made him forget that judging that the

* I have read in a book that treats of English genealogies that the Johnstones are subject to lunacy. When the Governor wrote the letter to which I refer, the phase of the moon affected him, apparently exciting a madness resembling the Bacchic.

glory of the success in the negotiations ought not be attributed to himself any more than to John Stuart, they concerted to accomplish my downfall by means whose knavery I am going to prove. The imposture once proved, they can only be covered by confusion.

As I am obliged to conform, in my reply, to the arrangement, or say rather the disarrangement of the articles of Governor Johnstone's letter, I shall reply briefly to the comparative observations that he makes on the tale of the Yahoos and turn his argument back upon him. I will say that if His Britannic Majesty pardons him this present extravagance, which proves that he joins to his impetuous temperament, of which all the world knows, a calumnious malice, I will say that if His Majesty pardons him, the poor colony which has been confided to him to foster, and of which he is the tyrant, will be quite exposed to inevitable destruction. The contents of my memorial will prove this.

"I put extraordinary value upon my time (he says) and very little on his &c."

He is ignorant, no doubt, that the governor does not have any time to himself, that he ought to employ every hour of the day hearing the representations, reading the memorials that each individual among the people who have been confided to him may present, and he has not known how to make good use of his time when he has employed it to render an iniquitous ruling founded on false and calumnious information which, I do not say is capable of dishonoring, but *ipso facto* does dishonor its author.

At this point I ask that enthusiastic spirit, what was the point of wishing to speak of the Count de Montault de Monberaut, of the Chevalier de Montault who is only ordinary M. de Monberaut? He compares these three names with the Holy Trinity from whom he ought to dread just vengeance for having designated it in a paper so full of deceit and calumny.

This gentleman thinks to do me great injury by treating me as a good Catholic. He ought not to be ignorant of the fact that I take honor in the profession of that religion. I have stated and written to him, I have written to His Excellency the Right Honorable General Gage, that the most advantageous prospects, riches, and honor are not capable of altering my faith on the least fundamental points of a religion that I find good and alone capable of procuring the salvation of man. I am entirely persuaded of the truth of the articles of faith which form the basis of that religion for whose support I pray God to furnish me occasion for shedding even the last drop of my blood. Governor Johnstone, pursuing his point, says, "who offers himself for a mediator and who has sacrificed all that he possessed for those poor Indians who are naked, &c." I shall pause here to reflect upon the dangers to which the human race has been exposed when savants put the catalogue of the flowers of rhetoric into the hands of the public.

When one recognizes Mr. Johnstone's ironic disposition, it is easy to perceive that that delicate flower is going to be mutilated and reduced to an unrecognizable state in such hands.

One can, from the little that he has read, recall that fable of Æsop in which that ingenious author describes a pretty little well-trained dog caressing his master and doing a thousand clever tricks before him which amuse him and merit applause on the part of the master, which he expresses by his caresses. The witty author shows us in *contrast* an ass which, seeing the reward with which the dog is paid, also wishes to share in the caresses, and to win them he comes at full tilt, braying in his ears and putting his hoof on his master's shoulder, which at the same time deafens and hurts him. Mr. Johnstone, who has read everything, knows what the ass's payment was.

I come now to Mr. Johnstone. He plays cleverly upon my *Catholicism* and on the expressions of which I have made use in dealing with the Indians in order to gain their confidence and to draw them into the English interest, the last point being proven by the treaties. I shall speak of that, however, elsewhere.

I am still speaking of my religion, as Mr. Johnstone attacks me at every turn on that article.

When Messrs. Johnstone and Stuart made their very impressive efforts to attract me to the service of the King of Great Britain, I had received the answer of His Excellency General Gage, who, with integrity and candor, pointed out to me that the religion which I profess would exclude me from all employment, especially military, in any place, wheresoever it might be, subject to English rule.

I showed that letter to Messrs. Johnstone and Stuart, telling them that, not wishing to remain in a foreign land in the status of a simple resident, I ought only to think of retiring as soon as I should have recovered my wealth. That reply gave them the idea of forming the most deceitful project that was ever born.

They told me, assuming an air of complete frankness, that in truth the laws of England exclude Catholics from all civil and military employment, but that they have at their disposal an employment which, being of new creation and uniquely relative to the Indians, cannot be subject to the laws made on the subject of religion; to which they added that since I did not wish to live in the status of a simple resident, the employment that they proposed to me was indeed suitable, that it was continuing, permanent, and capable of procuring me consideration throughout the province.

All that being proffered with an air of candor and accompanied by an assurance of continuation of regard &c., I was sufficiently taken in to ask them to make me their propositions in writing, and as is to be seen by the copy of their letter which I have put at the head of this memorial, which begins with a statement of admiration for the combat of passion and honor on the subject of religion, and love of fatherland, &c.

"Who even (he continues) has immolated his bullocks &c." As that trait is characteristic and preparatory to all the perfidies which since have been practiced on me, I ask those who read this mémoire to permit me to recount the facts as they have occurred.

Mr. John Stuart, Superintendent for the savages, having need of a great quantity of meat to feed the Indians whom he expected to attend the congress which he had convoked, undertook to place the arrangements for that provisioning with Mr. Blackwell, Collector, and concluded a bargain with him by which he would be obliged to pay twenty *piastres* for each animal that would be provided. Mr. Blackwell gave a share in the deal, in whole or in part, to Mr. Miller, nephew of Mr. Farmar.

As the congress was to be held in a hard season,* Mr. Stuart saw

* They thought to have the savages on the 15th of February. Several, in truth, came at the time indicated, but the congress was not even opened by the 1st of March.

clearly, shortly after having concluded his bargain, that it was impossible for the entrepreneurs to accomplish their engagements. I was at my estate when Mr. Stuart made that observation. He came there under the pretext of paying me a friendly visit, but in fact to try to engage me (as I have a considerable herd) to furnish him the quantity of animals which he needed. From the moment of his arrival, he made me a party to his embarrassment, asking me to aid him in the situation, by myself undertaking the furnishing of the necessary animals, saying that he would pay me the same price that he would have to pay those who should supply Mr. Blackwell, that is to say, twenty *piastres* per animal, cows as well as beeves. I told Mr. Stuart that not having been warned early, I had let my beasts scatter in the woods, that he was not ignorant that in the neighborhood of Mobile the animals were sometimes pastured more than eight to ten leagues distant from any settlement, that I would nonetheless seek every opportunity of giving him proof of my attachment, that it was enough that he appeared embarrassed to make me take great care to ease him, and I assured him that I would do my utmost in order that he should not lack food for the sustenance of the Indians. It was on this occasion that he told me that, wishing to keep a table suitable to the charge with which he was invested, he would have need of several calves, which he asked me to furnish.

Satisfied by the assurances that I gave of not leaving him lacking food during the congress, Mr. Stuart remained with me several days.

As his return trip had to be made by sea, I furnished him a boat and some negroes, by whom he wrote me the letter which is here copied (and I will be able, in case there is need, to show the original).

Copy of a letter from Mr. Stuart to the Cher de Monberaut

Mobile, 25 February 1765

SIR:

We arrived here at eight o'clock, where I found Colonel Wedderburn with three captains of the 34th regiment, all brave lads; Mr. Wedderburn is a refined and very intelligent man.

We have here forty Conchatys with Tomatle Mingo y Tibuet at their head; thus our troubles begin. There are several traders who say that in a few days we will have a great number of savages. Mr. Blackwell has already made provision for thirty animals in town. For the rest, we will entrust ourselves to the help that you can give us. The Choctaws have killed two Tallapoosas, and the latter have killed a Choctaw; thus those Nations are embroiled together.

I ask you to give my most sincere compliments to all your amiable family and know that I am, with the greatest and truest respect and consideration

Sir,
Your most humble, and
obedient servant
Signed John Stuart

The next day after receipt of that letter, Mr. John McGillivray came to my estate bringing me another letter from Mr. John Stuart which is here copied.

Copy of a second letter from Mr. John Stuart to the Chev[er] *de Monberaut*

Mobile, 27 February 1765

SIR:
I had the honor of writing you yesterday [sic] by your boat. A moment later, Mr. Blackwell came to tell me that he was obliged to get rid of the animals that he had in town because they were too thin for any service, and that they had all been sent to the woods, which obliges me to send Mr. McGillivray to talk with you and engage you to furnish the quantity that you judge proper sooner. I agree to everything which he will have the honor of saying to you, and am, with the greatest esteem,

Sir,
Your most humble and
obedient servant
Signed John Stuart

Mr. McGillivray, secretary to Mr. Stuart, provided with the authority of his master, offered to make a bargain with me for the cattle that I had. He made his proposition after having uttered some very dark epithets against Mr. Blackwell's proceedings, who, he said, had failed Mr. Stuart only in the hope of getting a better offer for his animals, but, he asserted, he would be deceived. I replied to him that, whether or not that had been Mr. Blackwell's intention, I would not abuse Mr. Stuart, in the position in which he found himself, who had already offered me twenty *piastres* for each animal which I should furnish; that I would be pleased on every occasion to give to Mr. Stuart evidence of the confidence that I have in him; that I asked him to assure him, and I will write the same things to him a little later, saying that I will never haggle with him, that he will always have at his disposal whatever I have to provide him. I will inform him at the same time that, in view of the rigorous winter that we are undergoing, it could be that my animals would be thin, but that he might be assured that he will have the best ones. I have given my word.

In consequence of the word that I had given, I took my best negroes and a white man to hunt for the animals, and I furnished the full amount that was needed. During all the time that the cold lasted, no one was envious of furnishing meat for the savages. Those who could trap some beasts killed them and sold them to the public. They sold the meat at one *escalin* a pound, and, as a consequence, made a greater profit from their animals than I, to whom only twenty *piastres* a head was offered. But as the congress lasted longer than had been counted on, Spring came, and the grass having sprouted everywhere, the beasts came in.

Then they all sought the protection of Mr. McGillivray, Mr. Stuart's secretary, who came, toward the middle of April, to ask me, in his master's behalf, the account of the animals that I had furnished. I gave him the receipts that I had received from the Storehouse. He went into his master's chamber and returned a moment later with an estimate from Mr. Stuart who allowed twenty *piastres* a head, except for six for which he wished to pay only fifteen *piastres* apiece.

As in that statement he had not mentioned fifteen calves that I had furnished, I made my representations concerning them to Mr. McGillivray who pretended that they ought to be given over and above the bargain, upon which I said to the secretary that I could give not one whatsoever above and beyond the bargain. He turned again into his master's chamber, who, he reported to me a little while later, consented to the payment for my calves.

I have since paid dearly for refusing to make the sacrifice of my calves. The furnishing of animals was taken from me and given to Messrs. Lind and Campbell, storekeepers, who did not have the proper people to collect them, and for that purpose they asked for Durand's herdsmen, who lent them on the offer of an ample recompense, which was made and which he has assured me has not been received.

I am by no means bothered by the deprivation of furnishing animals; far from it, it saves me from the responsibility.

The vindictive and self-interested Mr. Stuart and his domestics will punish me in the most sensitive place for an honest man.

In whatever company they may be, they do not cease to spread the worst gossip about me. McGillivray, under the pretext of making provision for grain for the savages, had been sent to New Orleans, from whence (coincidentally) he introduced into Mobile more contraband merchandise than grain. Was the merchandise for his own account or that of his master? On this the reader can draw such conjectures as he pleases. I know beyond doubt that Mr. Stuart was vitally interested that the batteaux bearing the grain should not be investigated.

McGillivray, then, who had some acquaintance at New Orleans, sent them defamatory libels against me.

There, then, is an end to Mr. Johnstone's irony when he said, "who immolated his bullocks &c." Before finishing that article, I ought to say that of the beasts which I have immolated, there are some still living: a few days before my departure from Mobile, I recognized two cows and two calves marked with the brand of Campbell the Store-keeper; I made my report to Mr. Pousset, police judge, and to Lieutenant-Colonel Wedderburn.

"From the state of these representations it is confessed that so strange a memorial did not proceed from what McGillivray said to Forneret &c."

I ingenuously avow, as Mr. Johnstone remarks, that the representation that I have made in common to him and to Mr. Stuart does not stem alone from what McGillivray had said to Forneret, and Forneret to my son. I have always recognized McGillivray as a despicable person whose gossip ought not cause a sensation; "it comes from the *froidure* that he and Mr. Stuart had shown me."

I will say, however, in passing, that he owes it to me to be grateful for the regard which I have for him and Mr. Stuart in giving the name of coolness to the knavish conduct which, I quite foresee, must have been terminated by the most manifest treachery. Thus he speaks truly when he says that that coolness, or better say knavery, was known to me when we parted, but he does not accuse me justly when he says that I would not have dared to uphold to his face the explanation contained in my memorial. I have, as far as I could, pursued just that explanation which he, in spite of his brutality, has not dared to uphold to my face. He ought to remind himself that one day, at Pensacola, he protested loudly against the importunities of the savages and said that they were continually intriguing &c. On which I said to him, in the presence of Colonel Wedderburn, "Several times, Sir, you have reiterated before me that the savages are continually intriguing. Do you suspect me of entering into intrigues with them prejudicial to the English interests?" To which he replied that I ought to know him well enough to realize that if he had had that suspicion, he would not have been roundabout in reproaching me with it. That response, blunt as it is, belies his accusation that I have not dared to sustain an explanation face to face. It belies also the imputations that he makes below, for that transpired either the day of or the day before the departure of The Mortar, who left last of the Alabama, Tallapoosa, Coweta, and Abihka, &c. Nations. I repeat it: I was present, as were most of those whom I will cite—for instance, Colonel Wedderburn, attached to the 22nd Regiment. I believe him to be too honorable not to be persuaded that if he is asked anything, he will speak the truth, whatever friendship there was between Mr. Johnstone and him.

I have many other proofs which will serve, no less than the first, to convict Mr. Johnstone of not being truthful in his charges, but I pass over them in silence, foreseeing that this memorial will be of a tedious length.

Mr. Johnstone also wrongly imputes to me having sent my memorial in the belief that Mr. Stuart would have left.

At the time of my departure from Pensacola, Mr. Stuart was there, awaiting the Store-keeper from Mobile, in order to regulate several matters which he had badly organized in that which is called settling accounts—*whether to the profit or to the detriment of the king,* I do not know. As I do not know how long that operation lasted, having written my joint letter as soon as I arrived at Mobile, I could as well believe Mr. Stuart still at Pensacola as believe him departed.

As for that which Mr. Johnstone pursues by saying, "I have acted in this fashion in the hope that some double intrigue which I might pursue would be palliated"—

I will reply that Mr. Johnstone does not do me justice in believing me so incautious as to pursue some double intrigue without hope of being recognized by some crown. In behalf of which would I be able to pursue it? Would it have been in behalf of the French? Mr. Johnstone is assured that I would not have been vouched for by Mr. Aubry, their commandant, who works with sincerity to maintain the good union between the two crowns, and Mr. Johnstone, in doubting my sentiments, suspects the sincerity of Mr. Aubry, with whom it would have been necessary that I be in accord. What is even more false is that all the French have taken offense at me for having written to him, a little while after, in these terms—

> "I believe, Sir, that you know me well enough to be persuaded that since I have decided to take service with the English, I will serve them, during all the time that I remain employed by them, with the same fidelity and the same sentiments of honor and of probity with which I served the King of France for the time he employed me."

Those sentiments are found extravagant in a man who has just left the service of France and who was in the position of asking—if not for himself, for some one of his children—to return to it.

Without pretending to blame those who have blamed me, I will say that these sentiments conformed to the rules of honor and to the circumstances in which I found myself. Thus, far from repenting for having expressed them, I thank God for having inspired me to write in those terms to Mr. Aubry since that single episode serves to prove the falsity of Mr. Johnstone's imputations. I shall have occasion in the rest of this memorial to speak more fully of his deceit and treachery.

I pass next to the article in which Mr. Johnstone plays Don Quixote and the hero of the piece when he says, "I would rather have at any time all the family of Monberauts, as great, powerful and numerous as they are, with the three crowns of England, France, and Spain, and also the Choctaws, Abihkas, Cowetas, and Tallapoosas my declared enemies, than any one a false friend."

That single fanfaronade characterizes the man and shows that he has become more worthy of the mad-house than of a government.

Did anyone ever see anything so insane as establishing a parallel between parties such as myself and my family and the crowns of England, France, and Spain, which he has no more shame than to put on a par with barbarians such as the Choctaws, Tallapoosas, Cowetas, Abihkas, &c.

You blind yourself, Mr. Johnstone; you believe yourself impregnable, covered by authority's shield; that aegis, more terrible to individuals than that of Minerva, is too heavy for hands as feeble as yours. It will indubitably escape from you.

If, when you are thus despoiled, some happy chance should bring us up against one another, you will hardly be redoubtable to a single one of the Monberauts whom you insult with arrogance, thinking yourself certain of impunity.

When Mr. Johnstone says that "I will find that he does not lack resolution to determine when he is pushed to the point, &c.," he proves that his fiery, brutal, and hot-headed temperament, which according to him was rather slow, did not permit the stroke of treachery, which Mr. Stuart and he had concerted against me, to have its effect.

In effect, when Mr. Johnstone says, "I thought that it would have been better, as I said to Mr. Stuart, to have awaited the decision of the ministry in England on your subject, so bad had your conduct been, &c."—he acknowledges that he and Mr. Stuart have painted my picture, which they have sent to the English ministry, with hideous blackness.

If the decision of the ministry had arrived before Mr. Johnstone's, it would have made the impressions thrown out against me, false and calumnious as they are, remain ineradicable, but I hope that at the sight of this memorial their Lordships, as well as the public, will be convinced that Mr. Johnstone and Mr. Stuart, true jay-birds seeking to adorn themselves with peacock plumes, only blacken me thus in order to throw more luster on the glory that they falsely appropriate to themselves, of having happily terminated the negotiations with the savages.

Your malice is very great, Messrs. Johnstone and Stuart; you know your interests, however evil. You ought to be content with appropriating to yourselves the glory which was due me. I would not have reclaimed it if, content to rob me thus, you had not tried to blacken my reputation.

Mr. Johnstone, continuing his infamous apostrophes, taxes me with an insatiable avarice. By what evidence has Mr. Johnstone thus recognized that I am avaricious? He has not always held that language. He has been heard on many occasions to extol my generosity; now it does not suit him to make public the signs of that generosity which Mr. Stuart and he have received. But I ought not pass over in silence the refusals I have made to countenancing the iniquitous means that they have proposed to me.

They cannot deny that, by the first letter that I wrote them, I said to them that being an enemy to all oblique means which many people use in order to amass wealth, I wished to remove myself far from any suspicion.

Notwithstanding so formal a declaration made to Messrs. Johnstone and Stuart, they cannot deny that (at the time that they sought to attach me to the English service) they offered to pad the expenses of the savages in order to find wherewithal to complete appointments better than those which they were authorized to give me.

My reply was that I did not wish to hold anything other than the king's good will, and that in consequence I would agree with whatever it pleased His Majesty to decide on that subject &c.

Mr. Stuart knows better than to deny that he offered to make a deal with me on the presents—a pretty pass!

The cold manner in which I replied to him has proved to him that he ought not make me such propositions. Does he wish to tempt me or engage me to pass over that which I saw daily? I know nothing of it.

Even Mr. Stuart will not deny, I think, that I sent him sixty *piastres* to be remitted to Carolina to Mr. Thomas's family. If I had been one to amass wealth by iniquitous ways, I would have appropriated to myself that sum which no person in the world could have known to be in my hands. I have even sacrificed my interests to my conscience, for I received £300 in bills which were worth only fifteen *piastres* of hard money. As I had made use of the deposit, I sent sixty *piastres gourdes.*

I shall hereafter have occasion to defend myself against the false imputation of insatiable avarice that has been made.

I pass next to the articles by which Mr. Johnstone violates the laws of nations, and above all the traditions of England, in order to adjudge by himself concerning that sort of man, necessary to the state, to whom the rights and privileges of an English citizen had been accorded, with the promise that he would enjoy them without trouble and without being bound by taking the oath of fidelity as a subject, while awaiting what the ministry had pronounced on the actual terms which His Majesty consented to make him. He cannot avoid just punishment for his infraction of the laws, especially when His Majesty or his ministers will have seen the proofs, which I have already given and those which it remains to give, that he is guided in his actions toward me only by the most criminal designs.

By the first article, Mr. Johnstone banished me from Mobile, ordering me to leave, if for Pensacola, three days after having received his letter dictated by iniquity and sustained by reasons as false as they are calumnious, serving as a defamatory arrêt—to which all this memorial serves as a reply, without making a separate article here. And if I should decide to leave for New Orleans, where he permits me to go, he gives me four days to make preparations for my trip.

By the second article, Mr. Johnstone deprives me of my employment &c.

Having up to now sufficiently shown the falsity of Mr. Johnstone's charges, I am going to render account of the reasons which have made me choose New Orleans, in preference to Pensacola, for my place of retreat.

1st By going to Pensacola, I would there have been subject to Mr. Johnstone's domination, who, in view of his capacity of judge and interested party, would have made me undergo new outrages. Those which I had already received were only too cutting and could only spur me to avoid those which would inevitably be mine by remaining under the domination of a man who, having an interest in debasing my person, would seize the opportunity, and by him I would be made to endure all sorts of ill-treatment with as much injustice and as little formality as he had taken in making the calumnious imputations on the basis of which he has issued a defamatory and ruinous arrêt.

One other consideration which estranged me from Pensacola is that savages come there daily, especially Tallapoosas, Abihkas, and Alabamas who are extremely attached to me; as at the congress they were told that I would remain in charge of their affairs, they have abounded at my domicile (so many that it was like being in prison). The savages could not find at my house any answers to the questions that they put to me; being desirous of knowing the cause, and not being able to ignore for long the fact that I had been deposed from my employment and treated as a criminal, they would not fail to murmur and would not, perhaps, limit themselves to murmuring. That is what Mr. Johnstone would have wished in order to take action to render my ruin inevitable.

These are the reasons which have determined me to retire to New Orleans, from whence I hope to set out for Europe as soon as it may be possible, to address my complaints to His Britannic Majesty or to his ministers, imploring their justice to make me triumph over the calumnies with which Mr. Johnstone and Mr.

Stuart have impugned me, to condemn them to make reparations for my honor and for my possessions which their injustice forced me to sell at a quarter of their value, without mentioning the awkwardness which my prompt removal has occasioned me &c.

I will also implore His Majesty's justice to have the conditions which I have stipulated in contracting the engagement with Messrs. Johnstone and Stuart, to which they have subscribed, executed in their entirety. If they have exceeded the powers which their instructions gave them, they ought to be responsible on their own accounts.

Monarchs, while able to punish the iniquity of persons whom they make trustees of their authority, are cautious of treaties which those persons contract in the name and for the good of their majesties' service.

If it were legal for a governor and a superintendent who, in order to advance the well-being of the state, have extreme need of a particular individual, to stipulate conditions with him in writing, and when that individual has rendered the service which was expected from him with honor and integrity, if it is permitted them, I say:

To deny the contents of the contract in order to remove from that individual all means of pursuit, to render him infamous, and to ruin him without giving any proof of that which is advanced, public faith would be banished from the kingdom; the governors and other people in authority would not find any person who was willing to render himself useful to the good of the state.

But as the monarch sitting on the throne of England has, without ceasing, raised his sword against criminals, infractors of just laws which are the support of the kingdom, I have every reason to be assured that Messrs. Johnstone and Stuart will be condemned to prove their allegations against me, and that being unable, they will be punished according to their iniquity.

I am going to place in a more obvious light the falsity of Mr. Johnstone's imputations, who, in order to give them more weight, quotes Mr. Stuart.

I will cite witnesses in my turn, of irreproachable weight and character, knowing the facts which have been published; to wit:

Admiral Sir William Burnaby and the captains and other officers of his squadron who were able to be present at the conferences of the congress;* the chaplains of Mobile and Pensacola; Colonel Wedderburn and the officers of the garrisons of Mobile and Pensacola; the Chief Justice and the King's Attorney General; Mr. MacPherson, Secretary of the Province; and other notables of Mobile and Pensacola.

As for the points which are made without evidence, I ought to appear more credible than my accusers who are already convicted of imposture.

Up to this point I have replied to that which Mr. Johnstone calls the preface to his letter. It remains to me to prove the falsehood of the charges of which the rest of this governor's letter, which he calls a reply to my memorial, is full.

Thus I am going to follow Mr. Johnstone article by article.

Art. 1 "Your son is a boy much spoiled by the natural inclination of his mind, by the haughty puffs and low intrigues of his acquaintances &c."

I leave it to respectable persons, to whom this memorial will be presented, to judge whether a son who learns that something prejudicial to the person of his father is being plotted is not obliged to give him warning. It is, however, that laudable action on the part of my son, which irritates Mr. Johnstone against him and makes him pour forth abuses more suitable to sailors who have disputed before the mast of a ship than customary among persons charged with employing people in an honorable way.

"Forneret (he says) has been a soldier, married a pretty woman &c. thus his mind is always fretfull &c."

Whatever the former capacity of Forneret has in common with the discourses which he says McGillivray held with him, the only question under discussion is whether these discourses are true or false. Mr. Johnstone supports them by the following.

Whatever may have been the reasons which made a pretty woman marry Forneret, whether it was ostentation or otherwise, he would wish to have her for himself alone; perhaps that is what enraged Mr. Johnstone. That is why he says that Forneret's mind

* Captain Carket hardly ever missed any.

is full of chagrin, but Forneret's chagrin does not stem solely from the addresses which he sees made to his wife; another object, more real for a poor man, impels him. Here it is.

Mr. Stuart, believing that Forneret would be useful to him, as much for his French secretary as to help at the store for the arrangement of presents for the savages, had engaged him at the rate of one *piastre* a day, a certain quantity of flour and meat a day, or a month, during the time that he would be employed, and had promised him, beyond that, a fixed gratuity to be received after the congress.

Forneret was at first employed at the store, but as Mr. Campbell, the store-keeper, operated differently from what Forneret thought he should, it was soon signified to him that he would be useless at the store, and Mr. Stuart decided to make him his French secretary. Forneret remained in town on the basis of being employed by Mr. Stuart for more than two months, at the end of which time, Mr. Stuart wished to give him only ten *piastres* in a lump sum. I do not know if the flour and the meat were paid to him. There is one of the causes of Forneret's chagrin.

"McGillivray," continues Mr. Johnstone, "has been a long time among the Creoles of Guadaloupe, &c."

Individual objects are not capable of sating Mr. Johnstone's rage. Hitherto he has defied all the Monberauts, the crowns of France, Spain and England, with all the Choctaws, Cowetas, Tallapoosas and Abihkas. Here he attacks the inhabitants of an entire province, for which he gives as sufficient cause McGillivray's evil inclinations and his delirium.

"However (he continues) on that occasion, it just so happens that he could pass for a prophet."

I do not believe that the prophecies of McGillivray are on a par with those of Daniel and other prophets of the Lord. They are, however, as sure—although founded on quite different principles. The latter predict the execution of God's decrees, and the former announce actions which must produce iniquity. In effect, McGillivray, chief servant of Mr. Stuart, whose secretary he is, knowing his master's secrets, and with whom I have heard him concerting and indicating the means of depriving me of my employment (of this I will say more below), could easily prophesy that he would fire me. If those are the prophecies in which Mr. Johnstone has faith or devotion, they are worthy of him.

Art. 2 I have already replied to the first section of this article when I explained the reasons which determined me to write to Messrs. Johnstone and Stuart demanding an explanation of McGillivray's remarks.

As to what Mr. Johnstone says of King Louis XIV's fistula, if I were a surgeon, I could give him the history of the progress which a fistula could make. I have had one, however, by which I was attacked when I was at Pensacola; that is perhaps why Mr. Johnstone brings the fistula into play, for I do not otherwise see what his point could be in speaking of it; but thank God, I am cured of mine, and the king, Louis le Grand, was also cured of his. As Mr. Johnstone draws conjectures against me from the fear which the Grand Monarch had that his malady was incurable, I can speak, as I should, from his cure and mine, drawing conjectures tending to hope that when His Britannic Majesty or his ministers shall be informed of the falsity of Mr. Johnstone's imputations, that wicked governor, ungrateful for the confidence which I have placed in his good offices, will be condemned to make reparations for my honor, indemnities for the loss which he has occasioned me in my possessions, and be punished according to the enormity of his crime.

As I have had no disposition of the King's business, McGillivray cannot have regulated any of my accounts relative to His Majesty's funds; thus I will reply to what Mr. Johnstone says here of the regulation of my accounts—to the article in which he speaks of pepper, salt and vinegar.

Art. 3 Beginning with the phrase: "that much patience &c."

In spite of the obscurity which reigns from one end of this paragraph to the other, it is to be seen that Mr. Johnstone wishes to say that, although he had not left me ignorant of the economy practiced by the ministry, I did everything possible to cause him and Mr. Stuart to make enormous expenditures, and that in order to succeed in that design, I unceasingly put the presents that the French made them before the chiefs' eyes.

I will begin my defense against that long and essential article by saying that I am astonished at constantly surprising a man in false charges who, because of his position, ought to be honesty itself; in whose hands the king has placed his authority that he might be the protector of truth. While punishing liars, punish yourself, Mr. Johnstone, for all the charges in your letter are false, and I can answer them in a few words by saying that so many lies added together make a total sum, and very considerable lies, like many additional pounds, finally number a million. It is quite necessary to detail certain facts which will serve as proof for others.

Messrs. Johnstone and Stuart, having commenced seeking me out to make me enter the English service, were after me unceasingly. We had several interviews together which often lasted well into the night. In the end they determined (at my request, to be sure) to make their propositions to me in writing, to which I made a reply which, not being accepted, put me under the necessity of making a second by which I left to His Majesty the decision of my appointments, those which were offered me appearing too modest.

Not wishing that the second reply should have the same fate as the first, before having it put in a final copy I communicated it to Mr. Johnstone who found it to conform to his designs and promised to ratify in their entirety all the conditions that I had stipulated. It was at that time that he told me, at my house, that I had omitted speaking of two essential articles, which were to mention the customs of the French and the expenditures which they made for the savages, in order, he said (as my letter was to be sent to the English ministry) to make known to them the necessity of making the same expenditure and to engage them to authorize proportional funds.

The other article concerning which Mr. Johnstone found that I had failed to speak, concerned me personally. It was the subject of my appointments, the augmentation of which I referred to His Majesty's or his ministry's decision, in view of the modesty of that which I had been offered. Mr. Johnstone told me that it was indispensable to establish reasons for my assertion that the appointments which they offered me were not sufficient for me to subsist on.

Not then being able to see that they were setting a trap for me, I inserted the two aforesaid articles. I thank Mr. Johnstone for contenting himself with heaping ridicule upon my narration of my expenses, both for clothing and for table. I will reply to it in its place.

Mr. Johnstone is not so reasonable on the subject of expenses. Having perhaps pushed them further than he ought, he seeks to attribute the blame for them to me, but I ought to be beyond reproach on that score: I have not made any. It is Mr. Stuart and he who have made them all, and what he says below, that I have pushed my intrigues with the interpreters in order to certify my accounts, is wrong. I have no account to certify! Mr. Stuart lodged with me, and if sometimes I have charged some goods from the store for the subsistence of the savages who came to eat with him and me, it was after having received the order for them from him. Thus Mr. Johnstone alleges falsely when he says that I have pushed my intrigues with the interpreters in order to certify my accounts. If Mr. Johnstone attacks that which I pointed out in my joint letter to him and Mr. Stuart, that I believe it was indispensable to facilitate their establishment of the colony and not to leave the new colonists exposed to the fury of the barbarians, to conform completely to the customs of the French, &c., I will say that before making it known to him, I had written the same thing to His Excellency, the Right Honorable General Gage, who has approved my system. I have since written to his lordship, Lord Adam Gordon, who has heaped praises on me. This I can show by their letters which I shall always preserve most carefully, they do me so much honor.

Mr. Johnstone, pretending, without a doubt, to be more enlightened than those two lords, blames that which they have approved; it is a sign of his discernment or of his malice which induces him to sacrifice the welfare of the state to speculations of a profit which will be to his personal benefit.

Mr. Johnstone accuses me "of having sought to render the savages' minds discontent and of displeasing them with their presents by puffing up that which the French ordinarily gave them, and maintaining the spirit of party among the chiefs."

That imputation is false, calumnious and instigated by the blackest malice. I wish that they would question all the savages who have come to the congress. I defy Mr. Johnstone to find a single one who says that I have held any of the conversations with him which are imputed to me; the interpreters can also be questioned. Not one will truthfully say that I have charged him to make the savages notice the difference between the French presents and those of the English.

Messrs. Johnstone and Stuart have never stopped saying, in the assemblies, that they would not take presents away from any of the former French partisans, provided that they recognize King George as their father, that he would only have to break those who would be rebels against such recognition; they wanted me to insert it in the exhortations that I made to the savages, and to insinuate to the chiefs formerly attached to the French party that all those who adopted King George would be continued in their presents, and that far from their diminishing anything that the French had been accustomed to giving them, there were some of them who could hope for augmentation. Those are nearly the terms which I used in my harangues, which, before being pronounced, had been communicated to Messrs. Johnstone and Stuart, for since I have accepted employment with the English, I have not written one word that I have not communicated to Mr. Johnstone or to Mr. Stuart.

The savages, to whom they had given hope that they would not encounter any diminution of their customary presents—and each one knowing to the very pin what he ought to receive—seeing that they would be much reduced,* complained to the interpreter. And as I know some words of their language, several addressed their complaints to me, asking me to set them forth to Mr. Stuart, which I did in the beginning, but seeing that he was probably better instructed than I in the needs of the savages, and not wishing to see him inveigh against the savages all the time and curse the givers of opinions in secret, I stopped presenting to him the complaints of the poor wretches who each, in truth, lost a little. But first one and then another sometimes makes a very great number.

* That could not be done without robbery, for Mr. Stuart told me that his list of presents entirely conformed to that of the French except for some increases that he had made.

I will cite events below, which will prove that Mr. Stuart could not have been ignorant of the extortion which is made on the presents. The facts, which I shall cite, will prove that it cannot be I who has, as Mr. Johnstone says, swollen his meaning in order to render the savages' minds discontent &c.

I do not know exactly what Mr. Johnstone wishes to say when he states "that he was convinced that it was a profit which made me accept, rather than a conscientious reduction of appointments &c." If he intends to speak of my refusal to agree to charge myself for the one hundred pounds sterling which he and Mr. Stuart offered me to spend for gifts to win over The Mortar, if it is, I say, of that hundred pounds sterling which Mr. Johnstone wishes to speak, he ought to have seen that I would have been able to make a profit there, for I am quite certain that I would have been able to content The Mortar better than Mr. Stuart and he have done, with an expenditure of less than £50 sterling; and it is to remove suspicion far from me that I have refused to be charged with the distribution of any presents. Messrs. Johnstone and Stuart well know, in the depths of their hearts, that I am unassailable on all points, and they can only base their grievances on falsehoods.

If Mr. Johnstone intended by that article to speak of the course I took of leaving the decision of fixing my appointments to the ministry, he is right in saying that I have hoped for some profit in the settling of my appointments; but my hopes were founded on an honorable means and not, as he suggests, on a means full of iniquity—for proof of which he accuses me of having presented accounts to Mr. Stuart wherein I show eight *piastres* every day for pepper, salt and vinegar, and, to heap ridicule on me, he compares me to an innkeeper of Canterbury &c.

For preliminary reply, I shall say—in order to appear entirely like the innkeeper of Canterbury—I ought to raise the error of the account; for all the accounts are explained, errors or omissions excepted, and to be able to demand the eight *piastres* for each plate, I ought to take into account lettuce, water cress and oil, which, joined with pepper, salt and vinegar, would make a good salad plate at eight *piastres*. But if I owe that error to Mr. Stuart, he owes me many eight-*piastres*, for there were so many plates on the table daily that an account of 354 *piastres* for the expenses of three months would not have been sufficient to pay; if each plate was worth eight *piastres*, each day ought to have produced many times eight *piastres*. —Thus Mr. Stuart complained to Mr. Johnstone that I had charged him eight *piastres* a day for pepper, salt and vinegar, and Mr. Johnstone, in order to compare me to the host of Canterbury, puts me in the right by asking Mr. Stuart to open his accounts again for the expenses of his table, for which he has paid me, for nearly three months, only 354 *piastres*, and I defy him to produce any account which he has paid me exceeding the aforesaid sum of 354 *piastres* and some *escalins*.

When I say that he has not paid another account than that showing that sum, I mention only that for the expenses of his table; for as I said above, I sacrificed myself in order to anticipate anything that could be advantageous to him. I have made considerable advances to him, for which I have disbursed my ready money; I have found myself, after his departure, somewhat indebted for some things for which I was run into debt by communication from him—of which he did not give me any accounting. For all the advances which I made to him, he forced me to take bills of exchange which I have had some trouble in having accepted by my creditors. If I had remained at Mobile, it would have been indispensable to have brought law suits. In order not to leave cause for murmuring behind me, I have been obliged, in order to pass my bills of exchange, to sell my house, with all the land &c., at a very low price, and to disburse my cash in order to give very extended credit to the purchasers, and to accept payments on which, in effect, they will make further profits.

I believe that the reader sees at present how ridiculous have been the complaints that Mr. Stuart has carried to Mr. Johnstone who, in his turn, draws an ignoble comparison. These two gentlemen do not deserve any other response from me than that which has just been read, which, since founded on true information, shows the absurdity of their imputations. However, their proceeding has produced effects of very great consequence for me, as one sees, in succession, the falsity and the iniquity of the means that were utilized to deprive me of my employment after the essential services which I have rendered. As the public and even my prosecutors well know, it is only due to my acceptance that the province enjoys tranquility. I am obliged to give the reader details which will prove my manner of thinking noble and disinterested, placed in contrast to that of my accusers whom he will recognize to be ignoble and full of deceit.

Mr. Stuart, Superintendent for Indian Affairs in five provinces, arrived at Mobile with the Governor of the Province of West Florida, December 1, 1764. The Governor was obliged to seek lodging with Mr. Telfair, merchant, who had gone to Carolina to purchase merchandise necessary to his business and might return any day; so his brother, guardian of the house and the rest of the merchandise, only consented to lodge the Governor on the promise that if the proprietor arrived with the merchandise, his lodging would be restored to him. Mr. Stuart was lodged with Mr. Crook, merchant, who had so little space that he gave his merchandise warehouse to Mr. Stuart for a bedroom.

After I had accepted a position with the English, believing myself fixed for at least a long time at Mobile, I proposed to assure myself of a lodging, and for that purpose I bought a little house which Mr. Campbell, Captain in the 34th Regiment, had for sale; as soon as I had made the acquisition, Mr. Stuart, who was badly housed in Mr. Crook's warehouse, asked to come to stay at my house. His proposition gave me a sensible pleasure; I then believed Mr. Stuart so estimable that I would have wished to transform my cottage into a palace, not for the profit which would be returned to me, but to be able to prove to Mr. Stuart my appreciation of the courtesy which he showed me and which I believed to be sincere.

Until the Governor's departure, Mr. Stuart remained in my little house—to the chimney of which, incidentally, he set fire. And all the thanks and indemnity he gave me was the advice to have it repaired.

The Indian congress being held later than expected, the Governor, judging his presence necessary at Pensacola, departed from Mobile about mid-January. Immediately on his departure, Mr. Stuart asked the younger Mr. Telfair for the lodging which the

Governor occupied on the same conditions: to evacuate it when his brother arrived.

Having accepted an employment that I had not asked for, but which Messrs. Johnstone and Stuart had offered me with eagerness accompanied by marks of greatest esteem, thinking those two gentlemen to be occupying places which are accorded only to persons steeped in sentiments of honor, incapable of any deceit, I believed, as I have said above, I was fixed for a long time at Mobile, and consequently I acquired a second house which was one of the more habitable in Mobile and more convenient to the operation which we had to execute, which was to hold a congress, as a consequence of which we had a multitude of savages with us continually.

Touched to see Mr. Stuart in an unsettled state scarcely suited to the dignity with which he was vested, as soon as I had acquired my house I offered to let him share my lodgings with me.

Several motives engaged me in that conduct:

1st. I wished to indicate to him my appreciation of the signs of affection which he gave me, which, unless one had undergone the arrows of his duplicity, it was impossible not to let him have.

2nd. Mr. Stuart and I ought to direct our operations during the congress in concert. We could easily do so by lodging together.

3rd. Mr. Stuart had testified to me his wish to conform to the usages of the French and to have at his house the means of having the chiefs and great warriors among the savages in to dine. I saw that he was without anyone capable of seconding his good intentions, and in fact, I had domestics for those operations.

4th. I spared Mr. Stuart infinite embarrassment by removing from him the trouble of disturbing himself if, every day, he had to prepare food for more than six or seven hundred savages who were to be found regularly at the hours of his dining—without counting a dozen Medal Chiefs and as many more guests of the town's notables whom he had to invite. Those, joined to the people in his suite, filled a table set with 25 or 30 places every day.

5th. In coming to my house, Mr. Stuart found himself delivered from the expense of a quantity of eating utensils, for all of his consisted in 12 silver spoons, two dozen knives with deer horn handles, 2 dozen forks with deer horn handles, three or four cloths, of which two were scarcely sufficient for covering an ordinary table, 2 silver and leather tankards for drinking beer, 4 crystal water carafes, two dozen glasses. He knew perfectly the use of the latter utensil, especially in the evening. He often passed the nights drinking, and Bacchic enthusiasm produced supernatural effects in him, for I have seen that man, who had scarcely been able to walk, so much is he afflicted with gout, I have seen him, I say, resembling a man bitten by a tarantula, excited by the sound of instruments, dance with extreme violence for a long time.

I ask pardon for that digression, which escaped me. I will not erase it, however; the trait is true. I have found it surprising. I believe that the reader would judge me not unwilling, upon occasion, to make known the character of the two men united for my ruin.

I shall return to my subject again by saying that Mr. Stuart accepted my offers with signs of satisfaction which I believed dictated by sentiments of gratitude.

I would never have thought that my conduct, which had been dictated by pure generosity, would one day serve as the basis for Mr. Stuart's infamous accusations and for the complaints which he carried to Governor Johnstone who himself had eaten rather frequently at my house, being invited by Mr. Stuart, and he had seen the sumptuousness with which that table was served, which he and everyone of consequence at Mobile had always praised highly. The words which the Messrs. Stuart, uncle and nephew, and his secretary, McGillivray (a servant as full of iniquity as his master) spread about incessantly, have necessitated my making public the accounts which I have presented to Mr. Stuart for the expense of my advances for his table. Colonel Wedderburn and several others to whom I have shown them, were not able to keep from showing their surprise at the modesty of the sums borne as expenses, and they have been rightly persuaded that I have made many omissions,* being unable to figure that 354 *piastres* could

* In enumerating the sums that I have received from Mr. Stuart himself, and of which I have made him advances, I have found that I have expended, since my acceptance of employment, more than 2,200 *piastres* of my own silver. I should not have had to stand any expense, for my family and I

suffice to furnish so delicate a fare in a land where a turkey gobbler costs 2 *piastres,* a chicken ½ *piastre,* a dozen eggs ½ *piastre,* a sheep 5 *piastres,* vegetables at prices so extraordinary that Mr. Charles Stuart, the superintendent's nephew, insulted an old French captain who made his living from the produce of his garden. Fish are sold at the pleasure of the fishermen who, knowing the need I had for them, sold them to me at extraordinary prices. I have believed it necessary to set out this detail in order to make the injustice of Mr. Stuart's proceeding known—who is also not ignorant of the fact that, at the very time of the congress, a jar of milk was worth one *piastre* in Mobile. He is an ingrate full of duplicity! That is what I shall prove, commencing with his ingratitude—I will say that it is great, for he cannot doubt that I was involved in extraordinary expenses on his account; not wishing to dishonor his position, I added to the utensils, of which I was passably provided for an ordinary individual, a quantity of others that I bought at great expense, and Mr. Stuart was not ignorant that during the whole time the congress lasted, the savages stole many utensils from my household. His domestics have also broken and stolen many. Mine have done as much and perhaps more. And not only has he not indemnified me for all my losses, but he has even wished to accuse me of having made considerable profits on the sum of 354 *piastres* which the statement shows that he has paid for his table expenses.

This circumstance, together with the other statements in this memorial, indubitably proves his ingratitude.

Now concerning his duplicity.

Mr. Stuart and I being daily on the point of leaving to go to hold the congress with the Tallapoosas, Cowetas, Alabamas, and Abihkas at Pensacola, I asked him to settle my account for his expenses with me. I presented it to him in two different statements, the first detailed for daily expenses, showing 172 *piastres* and 5

---

were to be nourished along with Mr. Stuart who, disregarding all the expense I went to for his consideration, had the indecency to announce that I have made considerable profit on the sum of 354 *piastres,* and to say to Mr. Johnstone that I have charged him 8 *piastres* a day for pepper, salt and vinegar, on account, in which it is easy for me to convict him of falsehood by the presentation of all the accounts that he has received, signed by me.

escalins; the second, for Frontignan wine, candles, and other articles not carried in the daily accounts, showed 182 *piastres;* the two together, 354 *piastres* and 5 *escalins*. Mr. Stuart, after having examined those accounts, was of the opinion that I should incorporate the last account into the first and carry the expense by days. For that purpose he ordered his first secretary, McGillivray, to indicate to the person who wrote for me, the form that the said account ought to have; that revision and Mr. Stuart's were accepted without the least contest.

Two days later I received news from my elder son, whom I had sent to the Tallapoosa, Coweta, Alabama, Abihka, Kashita and Chouanon Nations with a letter of invitation to The Mortar and other chiefs to come to take part in the congress set at Pensacola.

My son wrote to me, as well as to Mr. Stuart, of the good disposition into which my letter had put The Mortar and the other chiefs. As soon as I had read my letters, I went into Mr. Stuart's apartment, and located him in the quarters of his secretary, to whom he was eulogizing my influence over the savages' minds with a spiteful jealousy which was spread all over his face. McGillivray made efforts to console him, persuading him that it would be a new reason for him to bring about my destruction, &c.

They continued their conversation in front of me, fully persuaded that I could not understand English, but some words, caught here and there, easily made me understand the plots which were hatching against me. I made no semblance of understanding anything. I showed Mr. Stuart the letter that I had received from my son. He assured me that the one he had received from him contained the same things, word for word, after which I retired.

An instant later, McGillivray came to tell me that his master wished to make preparations for his departure. In order to set out for Pensacola, he wanted to wind up all his business in Mobile, consequently, he came to ask if my accounts were put in the order on which we had agreed. I handed them to him. He wanted to debate that account which had already suffered two revisions. I told him that having presented my accounts to Mr. Stuart himself, I only had to deal with him to settle and not to debate my account. The fellow replied to me with an impertinence which I would have corrected quickly if I had not feared to be lacking in respect for his master who, himself, perhaps, might have wished that I had resorted to some violence.

I had the good sense to avoid the trap.

Be that as it may, I immediately carried my complaints to Mr. Stuart who assured me that McGillivray had exceeded his orders, but as he did not reprimand his servant as he ought to have done, I resolved to write to him. In my letter I detailed the expenses in which I had involved myself in his behalf, for the indemnity of which the whole of my account would be a small matter. I reminded him of the sumptuousness with which his table had been served; I pointed out to him the indecencies which the people in his suite had committed, of which I had not spoken to him, believing that it had been because of lack of breeding that they had done them, but I clearly saw that they had actually been pushed by a spirit of malice. I finished by asking him to settle my account himself and not to subject me again to the impertinences of his secretary. I hoped that Mr. Stuart would make a reply or justification or explanation of his disposition toward me. I was deceived; he still had need of me. The Pensacola congress still had not been held. Perhaps he wished that I should not be there, and would have impeded me, if he had not feared to see himself held responsible for the lack of success in the negotiations, which surely would have miscarried if I had made the disagreeableness that I received at Mr. Stuart's hands known to the savages—for in spite of what I had suffered from Mr. Johnstone's brutality, I still had no reason to think him perfidious.

Mr. Stuart, not wishing to give me any means of justification nor to let me know the cause of his evil disposition toward me, made no response. He only told me through his kinsman, Charles Stuart, that he would settle my accounts at Pensacola.

The details which I have just set forth are long, but true, and I have abridged them in order to be less boring to the respectable persons to whom this memorial will be presented. They serve as answer to the article in which Mr. Johnstone reproaches me that McGillivray, in settling my accounts, recognized a transfer of funds that condemned me.

Yes, without a doubt, McGillivray recognized the means of my destruction. The first is a generosity which, sooner or later, will cause my ruin; the second is a good faith which can only occasion my destruction, having to deal with two perfidious men who had resolved to send me away as soon as they should no longer need me. That is what Mr. Charles Stuart, a long time before the thing was effected, had said to Mr. de Santilly, formerly an officer in the French forces, who has repeated it to me since I have withdrawn to New Orleans.

"I believe (says Mr. Johnstone) that one could easily find the proof, if this matter came to trial, that the public bread was sold by your family through the streets of Mobile."

I can only be astonished by the excesses of Mr. Johnstone's imputations, and I believe this one is as false as the others, for, of all my family, I had with me only my younger son, a lad thirteen and a half years old, whom I surely did not take along in order to sell bread in the streets. If, as a prank, he sold some bits of bread, it was, perhaps, only to the savages in order to obtain some bows and arrows; if he did that which I suggest, I protest not to have ever known anything of it, and if Mr. Stuart or his people had had any knowledge of it, they ought to have informed me. A few strokes of a whip, which I would have given the child, would have terminated that business.

If, however, by my family, Mr. Johnstone means my negroes, I had sixteen serving for the congress, to wit: four designated for supplying animals, and a dozen available for the service of Mr. Stuart or of the savages. For all of those employed by Mr. Stuart, he paid the hire of six negroes during the time the congress lasted; the others have been on my account. At every moment I encounter items susceptible to digression; I return again to my subject. If, by my family, Mr. Johnstone means my negroes, I will not hazard the assertion that some negroes would not have stolen some bread in order to sell it. If Messrs. Johnstone and Stuart had been sincere in their conduct toward me, if they learned that disorders prejudicial to the public good had been committed at my house, they should have warned me of it, and, in concert, we would have punished the guilty even unto death if the case had required it. But

Messrs. Johnstone and Stuart having never warned me of anything, I can conclude that that charge of Mr. Johnstone's is as false as the others.

Arts. 4, 5, and 6 The answer that I have made to the 3rd article of Mr. Johnstone's letter could serve for these, and my design is only to reply as succinctly as I can to the ironies of that governor who thinks to mortify me greatly by saying that a long time before he came to seek me &c. I had entered into negotiations with Mr. Robertson &c.

The negotiation in which I had entered with Mr. Robertson would have been of very little consequence if it had not been followed by an invitation on the part of General Gage which signified approbation of what I had said to Mr. Robertson: that I would enter the service of any crown only by virtue of the rank of colonel for myself, of captain for my elder son, and of lieutenant for my younger son; and Mr. Robertson, who had in his possession convincing proof of the confidence that the Indians had in me, thought himself obliged, as a good servant of the king, to engage the general to send me a letter of invitation.

After what I had said to Mr. Robertson, on receiving the letter from the general, I believed that His Excellency, disposed to procure for me the employments that I had indicated I wished, only wrote in order to put me in a position to make the request; and it was with that confidence that I candidly entered into great detail with His Excellency, which I shall not go into, however, since it merited his approbation. And Mr. Johnstone was wrong to treat as extravagant the request that I made for an employment which His Excellency avowed that I deserved and which was only refused me because it was not in his power to confer it, especially to a Catholic.

Mr. Johnstone, who has seen the letters that I have had the honor to write to the general and the replies that I have received from him, was wrong to make use of injurious expressions which certainly would be disapproved by His Excellency who, with all the politeness possible, in announcing to me that it was beyond his power to give me the rank that I asked, told me, "I do not, Sir, disapprove of that which you did me the honor of saying to me;

you have appeared to have all the sentiments of a man of honor and probity, which ought to procure you the love and esteem of everyone. In whatever land you may have decided to transport yourself, my sincere wishes for your happiness and that of your family accompany you; and if my services might be useful to you, I will be delighted by an occasion to prove to you how much I am, with great consideration &c. Signed: Tho. Gage."

Since His Excellency did me the honor of writing to me in those terms, he terminated the negotiation; moreover, his courtesies did not come, as Mr. Johnstone says, from the hope he had that I could render some service, but from the fact that His Excellency, full of sentiments of honor and integrity, could not blame a gallant man seeking to procure honorable positions for himself and for his family. And if, like Mr. Johnstone, His Excellency had been witness to the success of my services and the zeal and the fidelity with which I have conducted all my operations, His Excellency would have sought to procure me some recompense. Mr. Johnstone, to the contrary, works for my dishonor.

You have done well, Mr. Johnstone, but though your vices may be covered by the shield of authority, my innocence and my sentiments of honor will triumph over your calumnious perfidy. The King of England and his ministers are too just to leave all your crimes unpunished.

I have already said if Messrs. Johnstone and Stuart (acting with perfidy covered by a veil of good faith) had not offered me employment which they assured me was not incompatible with the profession of my religion &c., I would have retired immediately after having received the letter from His Excellency General Gage.

That general's letters do me such honor that they may be called the most telling evidence against Mr. Johnstone's reproaches, that I showed them to him in order to raise my own reputation.

I do not know in what book, or what place, Mr. Johnstone has seen "that a maid to a maid of honor that was not a maid was to get you the rank of colonel in Spain, how a secretary to an under-secretary who was no secretary was to get you a Croix de St. Louis in France."*

* Expressions in Mr. Johnstone's letter.

I thank Mr. Johnstone for doing me the honor of attributing to me a mode of expression whose sense I do not understand; I readily renounce what he can and ought to reclaim as belonging to him.

Mr. Johnstone reproaches me for having shown him a long branch of my genealogy since Adam. His expression "since Adam" certainly proves that he recognized in me an ancient descent from nobility that he ought to have respected.

His capacity (as the governor who made earnest entreaties to me to remain subject to England and to accept employment there) puts me under the necessity of proving to him that I was not born of the dregs of the people but am a man who reckons in the alliances of his house a Duc de Guienne, Comte de Bigorre, a King of Navarre, and one of Aragon, and who has connections with the ancient House of Bearn from which issued Jeanne d'Albret, mother of King Henry IV, founder of the ruling line in France. I could not, I say, dispense with showing him that a man allied to such illustrious houses could only expatriate himself if he were invested with honorable employment and with certainty of being preserved in his prerogatives of nobility.

If, when I had shown Mr. Johnstone my genealogy, he had made me the response that he attributes to himself, I would have seen what reliance to place on him, and I would have broken off all negotiations. He had too much need of me to speak to me in such terms.

I had already agreed that it was at my request that Messrs. Johnstone and Stuart made me their propositions in writing; I handled it thus because (if I may use some of Mr. Johnstone's expressions) I saw that our interviews were full of wind, and I wished to see the offers that were made to me clearly and to have the chance to establish (on incontestable grounds) those conditions on which I would decide to accept employment.

I have already proved that Mr. Johnstone employs the blackest malice when he seeks to turn to ridicule representations that he himself engaged me to make. I will observe yet again, that this gentleman is caught in false accusations in every word; if he wishes to give himself the trouble of re-reading my letter, he will see that in no part is mention made of my kitchen or my battery of cooks.

This same Mr. Johnstone (continuing his insults) says "that during the time when he treated with me, he recognized me for a man who was overcome with vanity."

I do not know by what trait Mr. Johnstone recognized that I was vain; I only endowed myself, at our interview, with things I was capable of doing and that I have since executed according to the expectations which I gave him.

Be that as it may, Mr. Johnstone is reprehensible, for, after having formed such an opinion of me, he did not break off all negotiation. I will be more sincere than he in saying freely that if I had had, I will not say the slightest notion, but even the least suspicion of his character, full of deceit and treachery—as he has given me all too convincing proofs—I would not have wished to hear any of his propositions. He would have learned (as I have grounds for thinking) of the sales which I had made of my goods and confiscated them if I had not accepted the employment which Mr. Stuart and he proposed to me.

Mr. Johnstone, as insincere on that occasion as on the others, claims, without any truth, "to have told me openly that he did not wish to have anything to do with me."

I have too delicate feelings, if he had held such a discourse with me, to wish to submit myself to a man who had spoken to me with such brutality; moreover, my greatest interest being in retiring, if I could without risk of being ruined, I would have seized that occasion if it had been offered me.

Mr. Stuart and he, far from proposing to break off, offered (as I have truthfully stated elsewhere) to pad my expense account with the savages in order to find an augmentation of my allowances. I have also made mention of the response which I made to them and of the position which I took of submitting to His Majesty's decision concerning the fixing of my said appointments.

Two objects determined me to accept the employment which Messrs. Johnstone and Stuart proposed to me: the first was the preservation of my property which, in spite of the sales which I had made, I feared might be in danger of confiscation—especially having Mr. Johnstone for a judge, who everyone knew was vindictive to the very end and who had engaged Mr. Blackwell not to pay me for that which I had sold to Admiral Burnaby. Secondly, I found occasion to prove to His Excellency General Gage that I deserved the praise and marks of esteem which he had shown me.

In view of the long time that Messrs. Johnstone and Stuart did business with me, I saw clearly that I had nothing to hope from them except the settlement that they would make with me. I recognized them for real Mexicans in their method of operation, but I would never have figured that they planned deeds of the blackest treachery against me. My great hope, therefore, was in the offers which His Excellency General Gage had made, to employ his good offices in my favor, and I have sought to merit his protection.

Lord Adam Gordon had also shown a great desire to have a conference with me on a trip which he made to Mobile. I proposed to find occasion to enter into relations with his Lordship, to whom I had the honor of writing as soon as I accepted employment. My letter contained a kind of memorial on my line of thought on the subject of the direction of operations with regard to Indians. My memorial conformed in every way to what I had said to Messrs. Johnstone and Stuart; it is that, however, which Mr. Johnstone takes for the foundation of his infamous apostrophes.

The reply which I received from Milord Adam Gordon is full of marks of approbation for my system and of his esteem for my person. He told me, in one paragraph of that letter which he did me the honor of writing: "I can assure you, sir, that it pains me greatly not to be able to profit from the advantage and the satisfaction which I would have found in the conversation of M. de Monberaut, whose sentiments do honor to the human race."

Mr. Johnstone cannot say that Milord's praises were in the hope of attracting me into the service of England. His letter was written after my acceptance and is, from one end to the other, full of expressions by which Milord congratulates his country on the acquisition which it has just made, of a subject as well intentioned as I am.

Milord Adam Gordon and His Excellency General Gage have involuntarily done me a very great evil: Milord in writing to me, His Excellency in writing to Mr. Stuart, have filled their letters with such great signs of satisfaction on my acceptance of employment, and with hopes which they had formed for success in the negotiations, that Messrs. Stuart and Johnstone have judged their glory obscured. I address myself today to these two lords, begging them to repair the involuntary evil which they have done me. It is to their glory to justify the fact that the judgment they have made of me is not false. I certify to them that, in spite of the iniquities of which I am accused, I am still worthy of their esteem. I have succumbed under the burden with which Mr. Johnstone's authority has viciously crushed me. As I have been put on a par with my accusers, I will provc that I have served His Britannic Majesty with honor, zeal, fidelity and disinterestedness, and that my opponents have formed accusations against me full of treachery and calumnies for which they deserve to be condemned to make reparation to my honor, indemnities for my losses which they have occasioned and to a rigorous punishment, serving as an example to everyone in office and proving to them that they ought not abuse the authority which has been confided to them only for punishing vice and rewarding virtue.

Mr. Johnstone's paragraph beginning with "matters being thus terminated &c." proves what his intentions were when he commenced treating with me and that what he has done ought not be surprising.

Art. 7 "I am sorry and mortified &c."

I am obliged to Mr. Johnstone for his recognition of the pain that envy has caused me, so that he mentions my enemies. I do not know if he who has adorned himself by plundering me was one of those of whom I have wished to speak; I do not know him to be one of the claimants; be that as it may, Mr. Johnstone differs from Mr. Stuart in this, that he has paid out of gratitude for the courtesy which Mr. Thierry did him in furnishing him a lodging, and Mr. Stuart bases his wretched proceedings on the same courtesies which I did him without their even being required, to which I have added, on my own account, a number of expenses that I have spared him, which are fallen on me as pure loss and ought to have been paid by him.

Mr. Johnstone wishes that God would make a great change in

me, and I only ask the Supreme Being to make me persevere in the sentiments of integrity, generosity and honor with which I have been filled even to this moment.

I will not only say, Mr. Johnstone, that I hope that God may convert you, but that the King may punish you for your disloyalty.

Art. 8 "Our choice has been so far vindicated that it was in your power to do some great service &c."

That characteristic article is preparatory to the calumnies that will be seen hatched in the following. It also serves as proof of what I have said above: that Messrs. Johnstone and Stuart, not content to appropriate the glory which was due me for the success in the negotiations with the savages, have wished to throw a greater luster on their operations by making it appear that the person whom His Excellency General Gage and Mr. Robertson had indicated to them as alone capable of making them succeed, was a traitor capable of working all sorts of evil if his arms had not been bound.

It is you, Messrs. Gage and Robertson, whom they attack by seeking to blacken the person whom you have designated; you have an interest in furnishing me the means of justification; your choice is justified. All the notables of Mobile, and of Pensacola as well, are aware that it was I who determined the savages, notably the Tallapoosas, Cowetas, Alabamas, Abihkas and the Choctaws of the Eastern Division to do everything that has operated to the advantage of the English. I have designated above the persons who were present at the conferences and can certify to the honor which the Indians gave me. Give me the opportunity of calling them to witness, particularly the interpreters Favre, Renochon, Germany, Forestal and Proctor. I also summon as witness the old trader of the village of the Pakanatalisi-Abihkas, as well as the other traders settled in the Nations, those who came to the congress as well as those who remained in the Nations but who have been witness to the operations that my elder son has executed in my name. Lieutenant Colonel Wedderburn has not missed any of the conferences in the two congresses. He understands French and English. He has served me as interpreter in the greater part of the individual conferences and in all that I have said in public to The Mortar and other Creek chiefs. He can give testimony that the chief who, Mr. Johnstone says (I believe falsely), made depositions against me, has given me credit both in public and in private, first, for his coming, second, for his acceptance of all the conditions to which he subscribed.

Arts. 9 and 10 "We have discovered that you do not have great influence nor were conversant with the Choctaws &c."

I have never claimed to have a great influence over the mind of the Choctaws. I can, however, say that I have served well in the operation of the congress. 1st. Without me, Tomatle Mingo, chief of the Seneachas [Ceneacha in Rowland—apparently a village], would have returned to his village without agreeing to be present at any conference or to receive any gifts.

If the harangues made by Tomatle Mingo, Alabama Mingo and Nachouba Mingo, the great Medal Chiefs of the Great Division and of the Six Villages, had been faithfully transcribed, it would be seen that they are full of evidence of satisfaction at seeing me at the head of their affairs. These chiefs have not failed to state, on every occasion, "that they had known me as the father of the red men; that their acceptance of new fathers in Messrs. Johnstone and Stuart did not make them reject their former father, who was I." I would never end if I were obliged to repeat, word for word, all that the different chiefs have said complimentary to me. Chulustamastabe himself, who is a chief always devoted to the English, was the one who gave me the most praise and who dictated the name that the savages gave me, which is like that of Mr. Johnstone whom they have named Mongoulachimataha, which is to say Prince of the Race of the Mongoulachas. They gave me that of Inhoulactimataha, which is to say, Prince of the Race of the Inhoulactas. The similarity of names given Mr. Johnstone and me offended him, without a doubt. That is why he seized the interpreter, whom he has treated scandalously. If, on that occasion, someone had complained of the interpreter, it should be I, for Alabama Mingo, premier great chief of the Choctaw Nation, wished my name to be Choctawoulactymataha, which is to say, Prince of the Choctaws and of the Inhoulactas, and the chief's interpreter imposed silence upon him when he expressed that opinion. I attributed that action of the interpreter to prudence and thought that he feared that Mr. Johnstone's seeing my savage name superior to his would only create jealousy against me, and I have never given him any other evidence of that alteration which he had made in the savages' kind intentions toward me, any more than the suppression that he has often brought about of the very flattering things that the savages said of me.

Before finishing the business of the interpreter, I ought to say that no one person has carried scandal as far as Mr. Johnstone does, for, on the same occasion on which he sent the calumnious and defamatory arrêt which he has pronounced against me, he arrested the aforesaid interpreter, named Favre, who was put in prison, where he remained a long time, then was transferred to Pensacola, where he also remained a long time without being able to have any means of clearing himself. He would still be in that embarrassment if the Attorney General, touched to see that unfortunate succumb under the weight of an unjust authority, had not furnished him the means* of withdrawing from his embarrassment. The Governor, seeing himself pressed to bring Favre's affair to judgment, went through the motions of giving some form to the charges which he made against him, but knowing the urgency of that man's joining his family, he dragged the affair out at length, and at the end of a time most certainly annoying for a man separated from his family and fearful of catching a contagious disease that then reigned in Pensacola, the said Favre was summoned to appear before the Governor alone, who put many questions to him, all tending to prove that he wanted some depositions from the interpreter against M. de Monberaut.

Upon the interpreter's assuring him that everything of which he accused me was false, the Governor replied that he saw clearly that he had not come with the intention of telling the truth. He then proposed to him to furnish two sureties, by means of which he would be allowed to return to Mobile and be reinstated in the functions of interpreter at Tombecbe. Favre replied that he did not want to be interpreter at Tombecbe, nor at Mobile, that he did not

* Parent, Favre's brother, has recounted to me all that follows concerning his brother's adventure.

have surety to give, that since he had become suspect, he was going to leave the province. The governor replied to him that he was not the master of quitting his interpretership thus, and ordered him to return to Mobile where, he assured him, he would be paid in the capacity of interpreter for time past, and continued until further notice.

I thought I ought to recount what I have learned of the interpreter's affair in order to prove all the iniquity that Mr. Johnstone employed, so as to shed some light of truth on the calumnies which he has set forth against me.

I ought not omit saying (in order to prove to Mr. Johnstone that my credit with the Choctaws is not so inconsiderable as he would like to have it thought) that since I have been at New Orleans, a Choctaw chief who is of no little standing came to tell me, "Since the English have broken you, I am going to break them." But not wishing that a quarrel between private individuals, or say rather Mr. Johnstone's treachery, which I regard here as private, should become fatal to the inhabitants of a whole province, I employed all the influence I have over that savage's mind in order to appease him by assuring him that I was going to carry my complaints to His Britannic Majesty, who would not approve of Mr. Johnstone's action. He promised me to attempt nothing.

I continue my reply to Mr. Johnstone; it may be permitted me to transpose a few of his periods, the arrangement of which puts more confusion into my response than there is in his.

"You have made some speeches for some of them to pronounce which we have traced to their source after they were delivered, &c."

Great is Mr. Johnstone's malice to reproach me today with having made speeches to the savages. He and all those to whom they had been communicated had given them their approbation. And if Messrs. Johnstone and Stuart had not pushed their treachery to the point of absconding with the copies of the discourses that they themselves asked of me, that they might be added to the reports of the congress that they had to make, if, I say, Messrs. Johnstone and Stuart have faithfully sent my harangues just as I delivered them and as they were pronounced to the Indians, His Majesty, his ministers and all to whom they may be communicated will see that a man could pass for mad who publicly spoke in the sense in which I have spoken, if in private he held to the same persons discourses tending to destroy his proposals.

I can prove by the attestations of Favre, the interpreter, and of Lieutenant Colonel Wedderburn that the harangues that I have had made to the savages are word for word like the copies that I have delivered to Messrs. Johnstone and Stuart. If they have altered them, I will produce some new copies and will present, if necessary, the originals. That made to the Choctaws ought to be in the hands of His Excellency General Gage, at least if Mr. Stuart has not removed it, together with the letter which I had the honor of writing to His Excellency. They tell me Mr. Stuart was charged to put my letters in the packets that he addressed to the general, and more than a month later, Forneret told me of having seen my letter to His Excellency on Mr. Stuart's table, who, if the thing is true, lacks good faith, whether he intended to prevent or to retard the delivery of my letter in which he well knew that the copy of my harangue was included.

Be that as it may, Messrs. Stuart and Johnstone cannot deny that the harangues have been pronounced. If they deny it, the attestations which are at the bottom of the originals will convince to the contrary, and if they do not suffice, I claim the public testimony of the inhabitants of Mobile and in particular of the respectable persons whom I have named above.

As my harangues are full of sentiments and exhortations to the Indians tending only to the good of the English nation, and as it is incontestable that they have been pronounced to the Indians, it is a strong presumption against Messrs. Johnstone and Stuart.

I beg His Britannic Majesty and his ministers to allow me to display my innocence in full light by confronting me with my accusers and their testimony, which they ought to produce in order to support their accusations.

If I were capable of that of which Mr. Johnstone accuses me, that of which Mr. Stuart has told him, as well as that which he advances on his own, I should be a miserable fellow who merits punishment, and I ought to find no refuge in any part of the earth. But if Messrs. Stuart and Johnstone are unable to prove their accusations against me, if it is proven that they are false, so they ought to be punished as grievously as I would have been if I had been found culpable.

The sword has been placed in the hands of kings in order that they may be the protectors of innocence and the punishers of crime. In order to aid themselves in bearing the burden of royalty, kings choose ministers in whose hands they deposit their authority and on whom they impose the same laws that they themselves impose. All of Europe eulogizes the integrity of the King of Great Britain, and that of his ministers, zealous protectors of the widow, orphan and of weak innocence oppressed. It is with confidence, therefore, that I throw myself at the feet of His Britannic Majesty and his ministers, begging them to accord me their protection in order to make my cause triumph. I am an unfortunate, bereft of good faith. In the circumstances that prevailed in the Province of Louisiana, especially in the Mobile area where the major portion of my property was situated, I could, without any compunction, embrace the English service or retire under the dominion of France. They have profited from the cruel position in which I found myself, having some property in the English lands and other in those set apart to France, which are today declared allotted to Spain. In that position, I have put off taking an oath as a subject, but before accepting employment, I proposed conditions to which they subscribed. I have served with zeal, honor, fidelity, and what is more, success more considerable than might have been hoped; I have merited some compensation. Not only do they refuse it to me, but they even seek to dishonor me by the most calumnious imputations, to render me infamous wherever I may go. And it is well known that indigent innocence has trouble making itself seen. I have been ruined by an arrêt which has banished me from the place where I have all my property, which I have been obliged to part with for whatever has been offered me on long-term credit. I will not say that I will never be paid, for if my purchasers be of bad faith, the authority of the law will oblige them to pay, but the least tardiness can only finish crushing me.

I have no need to repeat that the one who has carried out an arrêt so full of iniquity is Mr. Johnstone, Governor of West Florida, whom His Majesty has named to be the protector and father of the colonists whom he continually tyrannizes, and I am assured that several complaints against him have already been carried to the foot of the throne.

I repeat, therefore, it is against Governor Johnstone and Superintendent Stuart, whom he quotes in the letter serving the defamatory arrêt, that I implore, with an humble supplication, the protection and justice of His Britannic Majesty or of his ministers.

I continue my reply to Mr. Johnstone's charges; he says: "Having traced my speeches to their source after they had been delivered."

If Mr. Johnstone intends to say that after I had delivered a copy of my harangues to him, he had found there some condemnable things, I say 1st, that he injures himself, for my harangues had been in his hands for several days before being pronounced to the Indians. 2nd, I shall object that actually I ought no longer regard Mr. Johnstone as a competent judge of my actions until he presents my harangues before the tribunal which ought to judge him as well as me; if he does not wish to produce them, I will present them myself.

If Mr. Johnstone wishes to speak of certain changes that he forced me to make, I will say for my defense that I do not guarantee that my discourses have, in all points, conformed to all the regulations of a policy which it would not be extraordinary that I should not know well; but if all the contents of my harangue did not entirely conform to the English policy (a thing which I must take solely on Mr. Johnstone's word, for Mr. Stuart, who has lied several times, did not find anything there to change), if, therefore, something is wrong some place, it cannot be said that it did not tend from beginning to end to the good of the English nation, and the articles that Mr. Johnstone caused to be changed were, in their first state, at least as advantageous to the English as they have been since the changes indicated by Mr. Johnstone. It will be easy to judge the aspect of the phrases changed, as I am going to transcribe some as they were, and some as Mr. Johnstone put them.

Copy of a part of the harangue of the Chevalier de Monberaut to the Choctaws, as it was before the changes that Mr. Johnstone caused to be made.

In view of your former follies, my children, you are right to be ashamed; so also you ought to be most cognizant of the good will which the Kings of France, England and Spain have for you, who, touched by compassion for your circumstances, have conferred together and agreed that henceforth there will be only one white nation which can carry "talks" to your Nations. The King of France and Spain have ceded to that of England the lands which they possessed, which include your Nations, in order that he may more easily aid you and give you signs of his royal and paternal protection.

The same paragraph, as Mr. Johnstone wanted it to be said.

Thus you ought to be very cognizant of the good will which the King of England has for you, who, from the very moment he accepted the cession which the Kings of France and Spain have made him, named a governor of the province which has been ceded to him, which includes your Nation. He has also named a superintendent who will be solely occupied with the affairs of the red men. He has given orders to the governor and to the superintendent to give you signs of his royal and paternal good will and protection on every occasion.

Another paragraph of the same harangue, which Mr. Johnstone found susceptible to change.

(In speaking of the English) They show their attention even in having their "talks" carried to you by people whom they know to be agreeable to you. The Eng-

The other article as Mr. Johnstone had it put.

They show their attention even in removing every basis of suspicion from those who have always remained attached to the French party, and knowing that

lish, being informed of the confidence you have in Favre and Renochon, have taken them into their pay as interpreters.

Favre and Renochon are agreeable to them, they are going to carry their "talks" to you through them.

Copy of the only paragraph which has been found susceptible to change in my harangue to the Tallapoosas, Cowetas, Abihkas, Alabamas, &c.

My children, you have misunderstood the "talks" which have been made to you on that subject. The English do not demand your lands, they wish only to determine with you the limits of those which belong to them and which they have gotten from the Spaniards.

Mr. Johnstone required me to change "which they have gotten from the Spaniards" into that which follows:

They wish only to determine with you the limits of those which belong to them, which the Spaniards have been obliged to cede to them in exchange for others, as the English had conquered them.

The paragraphs transcribed above and elsewhere are the only ones which Mr. Johnstone found susceptible to change. His judges and mine will not find, I think, that what I wished to say to the savages was in any fashion contrary to the interests of the English nation and deserved the reproach which Mr. Johnstone made "of having traced my words even to their source."

I come to where he says to me that "I have made my efforts to sustain my reputation by making party distinctions, and, by means of a very scandalous interpretation, you have (he adds) abused the confidence which we had in you."

It is not I who have made that distinction of parties. It is the savages themselves who have made it; for no one can ignore the fact that the elders and warriors of the Eastern Division came more than a fortnight or three weeks after the departure of the two divisions, the Six Villages and the Western Division, known by the name of Great Division, and Mr. Johnstone, who said his presence was demanded by affairs at Pensacola, preferred going to regulate them to the accomplishment of his duties, which demanded that he be present at the entire negotiation with the whole Choctaw Nation. He did not see nor speak to any of the chiefs of the Eastern Division.

"With respect to the Eastern Division," he continues, "I was not present, but Mr. Stuart, whom I take for as honest and sincere a man as exists in the universe, told me that you had endeavoured to corrupt their friendly intentions, and to make a mountain out of a mole-hill, as was generally the case, and that it was only owing to his determined manner of acting, and throwing off all the frivolous matter which was brought to involve the simplest action in the greatest mystery, that he succeeded."

Before responding to that which Mr. Johnstone said that Mr. Stuart said to him, I am going to provide the narrative of what passed vis-à-vis the Eastern Division. On the first or second visit which the elders of the Eastern Division made to Mr. Stuart, he told them that all the chiefs and captains of the Great Division and the Six Villages had surrendered to him the gorgets and commissions which they had been given by the French, in order to secure others in King George's name; that he hoped the chiefs of the Eastern Division would do so as well. So abrupt a demand astonished the savages, and they showed their surprise by saying that "the English were like snakes who hide in the grass, lying in wait for travelers, and strike them on the leg, for the English do not give men time to know, until the pain comes; they made them repugnant propositions." They concluded by saying that they would consult among themselves and inform Mr. Stuart of their resolution on his proposition.

Mr. Stuart, who did not expect that resistance, appeared incensed by the comparison, but let it stand without reply on his part. It was made several times and always without reply. I was enraged, but I had nothing to say where Mr. Stuart was involved. The next day the interpreters came to announce that the savages' resolution was not to give up their medals, gorgets and commissions; upon which Mr. Stuart said that he would crush them all and give their medals, commissions and gorgets to others. As a zealous servant, I represented to him that his proceeding could have fatal results to the English nation. He remained, at McGillivray's persuasion, resolved to break those who did not sacrifice their marks of honor received from the French; upon which I asked his permission to go to speak to those chiefs. Having obtained it, I conveyed myself to the interpreters' house where they were. I was followed by Arthur Gordon, lawyer, justice of the peace and one of Mr. Stuart's secretaries.* Such a witness as he renders the discourses that I made to the savages—which I shall not report here, having pronounced them without any preparation, and conforming to the circumstance and to the sentiments of honor, of integrity, which I have always held, and from which I have never deviated—exempt from all suspicion. I will content myself by saying that not seeing any means of persuading these chiefs to the point at which Mr. Stuart wished to see them, I employed that means which is the sovereign mover of human action: self-interest. I announced their impending disaster to the chiefs. As pathetically as I could, I depicted the pain that I would suffer if, after having seen them dominant chiefs and the most respected of their Nation, I should see them objects of contempt in that Nation of which they had been the oracles. So I felt sick at terminating the conversation without seeing the chiefs determined to give the satisfaction that Mr. Stuart exacted; I saw them broken and without any hope.

The next day, Mr. Stuart (either being politic or truly desirous of going to take the country air) left with Lieutenant Colonel Wedderburn to go to the house of Mr. Morcier, Mr. Johnstone's counselor on appointments. They were absent two days, which I employed almost entirely in conferences with the chiefs who finally determined, and gave me their word, to surrender the medals, gorgets and commissions which they had received from the French to Mr. Stuart immediately upon his arrival.

That determination was not made without their previously having cited the evil treatment which the savages had received at different times from the English, and received daily from the traders scattered throughout the nation. The comparison of the serpent was cited again, and to it was added another no less mortifying for

* It cannot be alleged that Mr. Gordon does not understand French, for he was one of those whom Mr. Stuart had commissioned for recording the reports of the French interpreters.

the English: they said that the English were like crayfish which, when they see anything approaching them, hold out their arms and open their hands; those who take that action for a sign of friendship are the victims of it, for no sooner do they touch that open hand than they find themselves clutched by a firm grip. As I found myself in charge, vis-à-vis the savages, I turned their arguments against them and tore down their comparisons which has stunned Mr. Stuart who, ashamed of not having known how to reply to such puerile discourses, thereby conceived an increased jealousy against me which the eulogies of Lord Adam Gordon, and of General Gage, had kindled. Here, in a few words, is my response to the savages, scarcely less ingenious than their comparison, which I treated primarily as ignoble and insolent, having been made by indigent persons to their benefactors. I told them, then, that some maligners were like the animals they had mentioned; I was going to stir up some snakes and crayfish myself; if formerly, the English had enveloped my legs and hands with great bales of goods, I ought to be satisfied; that if the English were comparable to serpents, they were beneficial serpents which had in each fang pieces of cloth and linen which remained attached to the wound which they had made and should belong to the person bitten. That derisive comparison was made no more.

Upon Mr. Stuart's return, I rendered him a full account of what had passed and of the disposition in which the Indians appeared to be. He assembled them and interpreted to them the principal articles of the harangue to the two Divisions already paid off.* The chiefs spoke in their turn. The praises that they gave me were very embarrassing, being given before a person already full of jealousy against me because it was impossible for him ever again to call in doubt the influence that I had over the savages' minds. I certainly wish that all that the Indians said, in the different assemblies that were held for them in the two congresses, had been written down in good faith; His Majesty, his ministers, and all persons disposed to work for the good of the state would not be deceived and would clearly see what the Indians' sentiments are,

* The Six Villages and the Great Division.

and would also see the falsity of Messrs. Johnstone's and Stuart's imputations, who have joined together in order to make all the operations relative to the Indians appear only in such a light as renders themselves indispensable and puts them in a position to gain immense credit. That is the motive which has moved them. Court and town, instructed in the confidence that the savages have in me, could not fail to remark the difference between the superintendent and his deputy. The Governor, still less clever than the superintendent, has been regarded as a zero, not in regard to numbers, but in the head, consequently amounting to nothing.

That is why they are both united for my ruin, which would have been inevitable, as I have said, if the governor had followed the plan which he himself says he indicated to Mr. Stuart, which was to have my arrest pronounced by the English ministry.

The next day the chiefs and captains surrendered their medals, gorgets and commissions. The ceremony was begun by the captains and successively by the small Medal Chiefs, then those holding great medals, who numbered three, came all at one time. Their names were Mingo Emitta, called Tiou-oulacta, Tchouko-oulacta, and Mingo-houma. All three presented themselves together, detached their medals from their buttonholes with *sang froid,* then, taking them in both hands, they came, hailing me three times, each time bowing with the medal and with their bodies; they then went through the ceremony of placing their medals and commissions before Mr. Stuart. Tiou-oulacta harangued first, and the other two after. The *précis* of their discourse was "that they recognized Mr. Stuart for their father, representing King George. They then said that they declared that I had been their father, that the adoption they had just made of a new father in Mr. Stuart did not make them reject their former father, that on every occasion they would recognize me for their father, that the friendship that they saw existing between the English and me determined them more than all else to the conduct they had just entered upon, and that they were charmed to see me residing at Mobile in charge of their affairs."

I have promised above to make known by incontestable proofs the fact that Mr. Stuart could not be in doubt concerning the damage* which was done to the savages' expectations in the distribution of presents, and that in order for them to perceive it, it was not necessary (as Mr. Johnstone says) for me to enlarge upon the differences between the English presents and those of the French &c.

It is the knowledge of everyone in Mobile that Tiou-oulacta and the other elders said to Mr. Stuart at their arrival, and have not ceased to say, that in coming they had met their compatriots of the Two Divisions who were returning to their villages, and that they had found them, 1st, dying of starvation,† having been obliged to kill the white men's animals in order to subsist; 2nd, that all the chief warriors murmured much and complained greatly of the English presents, much less than those of the French in quality and quantity. Tiou-oulacta entered into the following details which surely have not been sent to court. Firstly, the *alconas,* or petticoats, of the women were so short that they could not cover their nakedness; the breeches of the men likewise so tight that they had trouble covering their nakedness; the *mitasses* so far from ample that the warriors' thighs were exposed; the Limbourg blankets very short; a great diminution in the quantity of powder and balls; and many of the other articles that he had asked his new father to give his orders for, so that the presents that had been made to them would conform entirely to those which the French were accustomed to make, were left out entirely; and above all, he had asked that although they had already given each of them two blankets, they should not be niggardly toward those who wished to attire themselves in full suits of scarlet.

In spite of the assurances that Mr. Stuart gave them that they would have cause to be content with him, Tiou-oulacta and all the others left complaining a great deal about the reduction which had been made in their presents as well as the articles that they had not been able to secure.

I come now to Mr. Johnstone's imputation which says "that Mr. Stuart, whom he considers as honest and sincere a man as exists in the universe, had said to him that I had used my efforts to corrupt the tender intentions of the Eastern Division."

* Not to speak of thefts which they suffered.

† They had been sent back without provisions.

Mr. Stuart ought only to be regarded in that affair as a miscreant or one incompetent in his employment. I have done, or I have not done that of which he accuses me; if I were culpable, he ought to have arrested me, made me defend myself, made me known to the savages as a man who deceived them and also deceived the English, and punished me according to the enormity of my crime. As I have not done that of which Mr. Stuart accuses me, he is a knavish, miserable calumniator who ought to be sequestered from the company of persons of honor and punished according to the enormity of the crime which he falsely imputes to me; and in this affair I take recourse anew in the authority of the King, or his ministers, protectors of innocence oppressed by persons vested with their authority and, as they are covered by that shield, consequently unassailable.

Art. 10 Commencing thus: "I must acquaint you that I am not insensible how far this kind of practice has been tried in order to impress, or to seek to play his game on The Mortar, & how far your son was instructed to write vain and false letters from that nation; but he is only a boy who ought to obey his father."

The same response that I have just made above to Mr. Stuart I ought to make to Mr. Johnstone; he merits the same treatment, his imposture being the same.

As to what he says of my son, I will prove by Mr. Wedderburn's depositions, if it please the King to call him in witness, that The Mortar has said that it was only my son and I who determined him to come to Pensacola. The letters that he wrote are true, and the imputation of Mr. Johnstone false; when my son followed my orders, he did well by the English nation. That I will prove by the results which he achieved, by following the instructions that I gave him. These instructions had been approved by Mr. Stuart and Mr. Johnstone, the latter of whom is in every instance surprised in self-contradiction. His slanderous fury carries him to the point that he forgets that writings of his own can be produced contradictory to his charges. I will cite below the *précis* of the harangues of The Mortar and of Mechtechiko which prove the errors of Mr. Johnstone's charge which I must follow exactly in disputing his statement "that he could not fail to remark that I had great merit in divining so surely where Topalga was, who was the instrument employed by me in order to make The Mortar come down, &c."

Having contracted arrangements with Messrs. Johnstone and Stuart, having accepted the employment that they had proposed to me, it was my duty to seek every means of aiding them in their operations. I could not doubt that their great aim was to attract The Mortar to the congress at Pensacola. To succeed in that, I informed myself as best I could of the region that each chief formerly known by me had chosen for his hunting ground, for I knew, and Messrs. Johnstone and Stuart knew, that The Mortar was with the Cherokees. Having learned that the said Topalga, a war chief very friendly and well thought of by The Mortar, was hunting in La Lacqu'une [the mouth of the Perdido River], which lies between Pensacola and Mobile, I formed the plan of attracting him to a conference with me, wishing to avail myself of him in order to get The Mortar. Messrs. Johnstone and Stuart consented to my project, which I put in execution by sending to the said Topalga, a savage Conchaty whom I found by chance at Mobile. The ridicule that Mr. Johnstone wishes to throw on the knowledge I had of the place where Topalga was, rebounds upon him, considering that the chief into whose care I confided my son served with zeal and success. Not only did he contribute much to the reversion of The Mortar to the English cause, but he even brought in a number of other chiefs and elders who were much opposed to them. He has been very badly rewarded, for not only have they given him only a small medal, but they have even mortified him by giving a great medal to a war chief who is much inferior to him in influence and in service. He has testified to his mortification; I have pointed it out to Messrs. Johnstone and Stuart who have said that what had been done had been at The Mortar's request. I cannot, with justice, say how the thing occurred, but knowing the friendship that exists between Topalga and The Mortar, I suggest, without fear of deceiving myself, that it was from bad understanding on the part of the interpreter or from jealousy on the part of Messrs. Stuart and Johnstone, who did not wish to honor Topalga whom they regard as my creature. And I assuredly know that The Mortar did not take it upon himself: 1. to demand that he should deliver the medals to them; 2. to give more distinction to Mechtechiko than to Topalga.

Messrs. Johnstone and Stuart have often reproached me that Topalga was very expensive. They will, perhaps, have also written to the ministry and to the General to this effect, to whom it is necessary that I make the bad faith of those two men known. In apprising them of all that has been given to Topalga, there has been very little in it for him, and nothing had been given him other than what is set forth hereafter, which has been approved by Messrs. Johnstone and Stuart who, at that time, would have given gifts to anyone in order to attract The Mortar, whom they feared with reason, to the congress and to their cause.

After Topalga accepted the commission that I gave him, and had listened attentively to what Messrs. Johnstone and Stuart, who at that time held a more humble language than that which they hold today, said to him, he responded that "he was disposed to obey the orders of his 'father' (who was me) in everything"; that since I told him that it was necessary "to bury all of the bad 'talks' of old times, which were no longer valid, in favor of new ones which would be substituted, which were good—which he understood—" that he would go inform The Mortar and the other chiefs; that he would ask their new fathers, Messrs. Johnstone and Stuart, to consider that the riches of the red men consisted in their hunting; that he had with him many warriors who would not abandon it; and that he could not give it up; that he thought it indispensable in their fathers "to indemnify those people who were going to abandon all in order to carry on their 'talks'." He represented that the English reaped two advantages in satisfying their demands: the first, of doing an act of justice; the second, of putting those who thus received presents in the position of extolling the generosity of the English, which would have a very good effect in the Nation. He then established the body of their demands, detailing what he would demand for each of his warriors and Messrs. Stuart and Johnstone, then very respectful toward me, charged me to give to the store-keeper the statement of what he should distribute.

I figure that what I have just said, which is true, proves the absurdity of Mr. Johnstone's irony, since he says that I knew where Topalga was and that I ought to confess that his presents had some effect in bringing about his cooperation. He is also contradicted in this particular by what he says in the following: that "The Mortar himself avowed in public that it was principally by Mr. Struthers' persuasion that he came down," and that I had asked him several times to say that it was by my orders that he had come, and that he had not wished to do it.

Mr. Johnstone's charge is false in every point. 1. The Mortar never made that avowal in public. That is easily determined by the testimony of the interpreters, of Colonel Wedderburn, of the Admiral and of all the other notable persons whom I have cited above; all the different estates, whether military or civil, ecclesiastics, judges, merchants and artisans of Pensacola, who have heard The Mortar's depositions, regard me as the guardian who delivered them from the savages' tyranny. I beg Mr. Johnstone to say in what assembly, in what place The Mortar publicly confessed that he came down at Mr. Struthers' persuasion. I think that Mr. Johnstone will be most embarrassed when it becomes necessary that he give proof of what he advances as lightly as he does falsely. I can, on the other hand, prove by several of The Mortar's public depositions (some harangues which I shall cite below in *précis)* that he did not cease rendering me signs of his affection and that, very far from saying that I solicited him to say that he only came down at my invitation, but that he had not wanted to do so, he did not cease saying that, rejecting all the invitations that had been made to him from Charlestown, from Virginia, from Pensacola, from Mobile, he had acceded only to mine; that seeing it seconded by the envoy that I had made of my son, he was not able to doubt the sincerity of my request, &c.

Mr. Stuart is unable to deny that my son being with him and the old trader of the village of Pakanatalisi, that man, accomplished in Indian politics, took my son by the hand and flattered him in every way and presented him to Mr. Stuart, saying to him, "There is the gentleman who has led The Mortar and all the other chiefs and Creek notables here; I have been witness to the zeal with which he employed himself for the success of his mission. Without him you would have seen here neither The Mortar nor any red man. To substantiate what I say, pay attention to what The Mortar and the others constantly tell you." Mr. Stuart and McGillivray wanted him to say that the other Englishmen sent into the Nation had more part than my son in the coming of The Mortar and the others and in their good dispositions. "No," the old trader replied, "those who have been sent into the Nation the savages have only rebuffed; all would have miscarried if that gentleman had not set the spoiled affairs aright, and you can count on it that he and his father will always gain more over the Indians' minds with three rolls of tobacco than you and all those whom you can send would know how to do with fifty pieces of Limbourg."

If Mr. Johnstone did not know of that event, he could have learned it from Mr. Stuart.

When The Mortar left Pensacola, I was still there and did not leave until eight days after The Mortar. The discourse which Mr. Johnstone attributes to that chief had not then transpired; no one had heard it spoken. Colonel Wedderburn himself, who did not leave Mr. Johnstone and Stuart, assured me of never having heard it spoken in the time that he was in Pensacola. Thus what Mr. Johnstone says is false—that The Mortar made his deposition in public.

But I wonder if The Mortar, excited and corrupted by someone, would have been able to hold such speech? Why is it that Mr. Johnstone puts faith in testimony that everyone is ignorant of, and himself wishes to ignore the numerous depositions made with the greatest possible authenticity?

Can Mr. Johnstone be unaware that The Mortar, some days before his departure, came into my chamber to present me the letter that I had written him, telling me that it had only been that letter and the sight of my son that had determined him to come, &c. Colonel Wedderburn had the kindness to explain the interpreters' report to me. Thus he can give testimony to the marks of confidence which The Mortar gave to me.

I could have made good use of the French interpreter Renochon, but wishing, in case of need, to have irreproachable testimony, and as I found Colonel Wedderburn disposed to explain the interpreters' report, I made use of the English. I did not forsee that Mr. Johnstone would falsely attribute The Mortar's decision to Mr. Struthers, and that the same Mr. Johnstone would say, also falsely, that The Mortar had said in public that I had solicited him through Topalga to say that it was by my orders that he had come, and that he had not wanted to do so. I have said it, and I repeat it: The Mortar never did make that deposition in public. If he had, it would not have been unknown to everyone. Colonel Wedderburn especially would have known of it, and when Mr. Johnstone's defamatory arrêt was made, he was most astounded by that charge. The deposition not having been made in public, as Mr. Johnstone says, I can only conclude that what he has charged is false.

Besides, could Mr. Johnstone doubt the sentiments of the Nation in my regard? Does he not remember that upon a difficulty occasioned by the pillage of some merchandise, Messrs. Hannay and Campbell sent some couriers and the savages some deputies; the savages' deputies said, in their discourse in the name of the chiefs who had sent them that they "had learned with pleasure" that their "father was in Mobile, seated beside the English chiefs"; that they had believed their father dead or lost to them, but that they "had seen his flesh* who" had assured them that he was still alive, that he would await them; that they "would consider coming down to shake hands" with their father and "speaking to him" from the bottom of their hearts. These, roughly, were the expressions of the savages' deputy from the village of the Talisis. Mr. Johnstone had written that deposition well anterior to the negotiations of Struthers, who was still at Mobile and only left on the news that the couriers brought him, that the stolen merchandise was from his warehouses. Before setting out, Struthers, going to take leave of Mr. Johnstone, offered him his services. Mr. Johnstone has told me that he replied to him, "Sir, I do not expect nor ask any service of you. I only ask you not to traverse the operations of the people whom we have sent."

After such a response, Struthers would not be expected to become the spoiler of the success of the negotiations.

* Savage expression which means his son.

"I can never think I owe so great an obligation to your son as you seem to make out, though I shall not lessen the reward which I have recommended to the government. Your son was well fed, well cared for, and better paid than his father ever was for the commission which he bore while he was in the French service, &c."

Mr. Johnstone holds a rancor without equal against my son whom, however, he has recognized in his letter as being worthy of the esteem of illustrious persons, &c.

Mr. Johnstone has so great a desire to say injurious things that he does not perceive that he says them against himself and declares himself a liar before the ministry in the charges that he made against my son, who has merited or has not merited the compensation that Mr. Johnstone has demanded for him. When Mr. Johnstone wrote, he could not fail to know what my son's merits were. His letter was written after the congress, at least if it is that which he read to Mr. Stuart, Colonel Wedderburn, my son and me. I deceive myself; perhaps it is not that which he read to us, for he sought to persuade the ministry that it would be necessary to reduce the savages by force. Mr. Stuart having conferred with me on that point, I said conscientiously that it would be contrary to the welfare of the state, and Mr. Stuart assured me that he would not sign it so long as that point remained; and Colonel Wedderburn has told me since that the article had been changed. All the rest of the charges in that letter prove that it was written after the congress ended, since Mr. Johnstone says to His Lordship that he will be in a position to judge for himself by the appearance of the details of the operations &c. The congress being finished, Mr. Johnstone therefore knew what my son's merits were, and Mr. Stuart and he, having judged him worth a reward which exceeded their authority, they jointly demanded it from the government. There is most evident proof of the falsity of the imputations that Mr. Johnstone makes against my son whom he also improperly says to have been well fed, well cared for and better paid &c.

During the entire time he was with the savages, my son was badly fed, had no other guard than my credit among the Nations, which in truth was worth more to him than all the satellites that Mr. Johnstone might have been able to give him. As for payment, if the government accords my son the gratification of one hundred pounds sterling which Messrs. Johnstone and Stuart told me they requested for him, he would not have cause for complaining of the treatment that was given him. It is proper to state, however, that he has been deceived, for he had much less than that which was promised to him, independent of the gratifications and other gifts which they had promised to procure for him from the government. But as all these promises were verbal, it was useless to demand them from two persons of such bad faith as Messrs. Johnstone and Stuart who, in that affair, appear as both judges and parties.

The following words, up to Article Eleven, only attack my small fortune without assailing my reputation and only deserve a show of disdain on my part.

Art. 11 commences thus: "You pressed your service or that &c. to go out to meet the Creeks, and Colonel Wedderburn was generous enough to accompany you &c."

It would seem, seeing how Mr. Johnstone reproaches me, that I anticipated the Creeks in spite of him. However, he offered me his chair for that little trip—proof of his consent. I will have boundless appreciation all my life for the generosity which Colonel Wedderburn showed in coming with me to confront the Creeks. His conduct is laudable in every respect. He proves (1)—in spite of indications, which he could not fail to see, of those traits of perfidy which are attributed to me—that he is delighted to find occasion to be able to give testimony, any time, of the innocence of a gallant man whom he sees at the point of succumbing to the weight of an authority full of iniquity. In the second place, Mr. Wedderburn would give proof of his zeal for the service of his King by closely following an operation which, contrary to Governor Johnstone's treatment as a silly comedy, ought to be, and was, as glorious to the English nation as working in conjunction with the Indians can be to a European nation. That is what I will prove and what my illustrious judges will recognize from the details which I will unceasingly present. It is first necessary that I render account of the reasons that caused me to entreat Colonel Wedderburn to come with me to the meeting with The Mortar and with all the chiefs, war chiefs and warriors of the Abihka, Alabama, Tallapoosa, Coweta and Chouanon Nations. I was not ignorant that jealousy possessed Mr. Stuart's heart, animated him against me so as to make him seek every means of ruining me. I had promised him not to see the savages before him; however, while he and I were returning to Pensacola, the situation changed. I had ample knowledge that the savages were full of roguish plots. I wished to engage them to present themselves to the English only in a posture (if not altogether of humility) at least full of decency. I could have expired in my little enterprise, and if I had not succeeded, what would they not have said since they reproach me after my success!

In that perplexity of ideas, I seek to have for witness to the sincerity of my conduct, a person who by his character can impose silence upon that calumny so much the more to be feared as it is clad in the armor of authority.

I have known only sentiments of integrity, honor and probity in Mr. Wedderburn, which, added to an ardent zeal that he possesses for rendering himself useful in all the work of the service, made me hope that he would not refuse to accompany me in going before The Mortar and the other chiefs. With prayers I made him the proposition, to which I added this: as he spoke French very well, I wished him to explain to the English interpreters what I was going to say to the Indians, and Mr. Wedderburn did me a most sensible pleasure when he granted me his consent. It ought to be recalled that en route I told him everything of which I was aware concerning Mr. Stuart's jealousy, and I made him a recital of what I had heard of the plots which Mr. Stuart made against me, having surprised him, as I have said above, holding counsel with his secretaries; persuaded as they were that I did not understand a word of English, they were not embarrassed before me.

I could not have a better witness to my innocence than Colonel Wedderburn.

Toward the end of March or in the first days of April, some Tallapoosa Indians murdered a white man on the road which led from Pensacola to Mobile. The news of the murder reached the Nation while my son pressed the chiefs for a decision to be present at the Pensacola congress, and when for final decision they only awaited the arrival of The Mortar. The Indians, always suspicious and asking others what they thought, fearing that the English would take vengeance for bloodshed on those who would come to the congress—whether by trickery or otherwise—implored my son to send couriers to ascertain what the English attitude would be on that subject; and the couriers were bearers of all the signs of peace used by the savages, which they addressed to Mr. Stuart and to me. By return couriers I sent my son a speech to interpret to the Indians in which I reproached the license of their young men. I exhorted them most pathetically to excite the influential men to put a check on that license. I did not promise the expunction of the crime, but I assured them that they could come with all surety, without having to fear any reprisal upon those who would come. This memorial is already too long; therefore, I will not insert any of my discourses to the savages which, however, I will present if it is necessary. They have all gained general approbation and especially that of Messrs. Johnstone and Stuart; and he whom Mr. Johnstone blames in that Article has not been found otherwise subject to censure except from a fear that the savages might be scandalized by the reproaches I made to them for their license. The results have proved that if the savages have testified to the sensibleness of my reproaches, they have with docility, adopted the means I have proposed to them for repairing their faults. I will prove that by the following: by the narrative of the conduct that Mr. Johnstone treats as comedy. My little harangue being made on the plan set forth above, I communicated it to Mr. Stuart who approved it so strongly that he wrote nothing to my son other than to follow his father's orders step by step. I will interrupt myself a bit, here, in order to observe that the orders of that father were not as dangerous as Mr. Johnstone indicates above. I also have in hand some letters from him which order my son to conform to my orders.

As Mr. Johnstone was at Pensacola, and as Mr. Stuart wished to decide nothing alone in an affair which was solely relative to the Province, he ordered the couriers to pass through Pensacola to get Mr. Johnstone's orders. I also wrote and, in an open letter, addressed despatches for my son to him, asking him to augment or diminish in my harangue that which he found either too little or too much. At the same time I gave him the details of the part I had played in the work with the Eastern Division of the Choctaws, and of the indications of attachment which the chiefs had given me, &c. I communicated my letter to Mr. Stuart.*

The detour which had to be made so that the couriers could pass through Pensacola (together with the fact that Mr. Stuart, finding the affair of great consequence, did not send them on promptly) consumed a considerable time, during which my son, having found The Mortar in a good mood, brought him to the resolution of fixing the day of his departure and relayed that news to us. At the same time I was informed by the couriers that the savages had no intention of backing down before the English; whether the murderers were granted or refused pardon (and assuming that in either case their fate was already settled), the Indians were firmly resolved to give themselves as little trouble as possible and not to hand them over.

As for the murdered man, he was a French deserter, a bad actor who, having insulted the savages, had, in a fashion, merited the results of their vengeance, and had been executed by a sort of assassination. But the savages had no other method of executing their vengeance.

Examining all maturely, I communicated the project which I had formed to Messrs. Johnstone and Stuart: if they were of a mind to grant oblivion to the crime, to lead the savages to them in a suppliant posture, asking pardon for the guilty. As I have truthfully stated above, Mr. Johnstone, to whom I communicated the little discourse that I proposed making to the savages, found nothing to change. He only showed fear that offense would be taken at the painful reproaches that I would make to them. I told him that I certainly expected some murmuring, but that I believed myself sure of succeeding; that whatever might be the result of my conduct, the blame (if there were any) could only fall on me.

* If, as Mr. Johnstone says that Mr. Stuart said to him, he thought that I sought to corrupt the kindly intentions of those chiefs, he ought not have allowed me the advantage, before the Governor, of having contributed to the welfare of the operations. Mr. Stuart was well assured of the fidelity with which I served, and in each line I have written are found circumstances proving that Mr. Johnstone and Stuart are a pair of calumniators.

In the event that I succeeded, the proceedings would be glorious for the English nation. I ask Mr. Johnstone if these can come from a traitor?

I come to the particulars of what took place at my interview with the savages, and I call Colonel Wedderburn as witness to certify to the truth of my account. There were also present the two interpreters, Renochon and Forestal, and Mr. Maclellan, today deputy secretary of the Province, and many of the military attended, with whom I am not acquainted.

The savages were camped in a valley formed by a small stream. As soon as the sedan-chair in which I traveled with the Colonel appeared at the summit of the hill, they sent to beg me to halt, and The Mortar detached the most important chiefs after himself to receive me with the greatest marks of honor which the savages can give.

The Mortar's deputies made me, on his behalf, some small compliments, saying that he was going to be charmed to see his "father" again, whom he had believed dead and whom he had been told he would never see again, after which they presented to me a rod to which two peace pipes were attached. I took the Colonel's hand, which I placed with mine on the staff, saying to the savages that this gentleman was a great warrior, commander of troops, and my special friend. That ceremony concluded, two chiefs took me by each arm; two others did the same with the Colonel, and singing songs of peace, led us in triumph to the camp where The Mortar awaited us under a large shelter which he had had made, not without great efforts, from leafy branches. The marks of friendship which we exchanged were very affectionate on his part; I will say on mine also. He also received the Colonel with evidence that he thought well of his "father's" friend.

I caused the speech, which Mr. Johnstone says to have been improper, to be interpreted to the savages. He is wrong in stating that the savages, disgusted at the first sentence, refused to hear it, and we were not aware of the repugnance which some young men had on hearing my reproaches. As the interpreter displayed unwarranted timidity, I persisted in requiring him to interpret it to them. I can certify that The Mortar and several other chiefs heard it to the end, not only without murmur, but even giving signs of approbation at the end of each phrase.

When I had finished speaking, the chiefs assembled together to consider the reply which they would give me through Mechtechiko (then carrying "talks" for The Mortar; today a chief, therefore holding a great medal). Here it is in substance: The Mortar and all the chiefs were very happy to see their "father" whom they had believed lost. The Mortar had been invited from Charlestown, Savannah, Georgia, Virginia, Mobile, Pensacola, to go hear speeches, but he had not wished to accept any of these invitations. Finally his "father" had sent him word, which had been carried to him by his "father's" own flesh and blood; then he was moved to come to hear his "father's" word. He should not be astonished at hearing the grumbling of children who had lost heart; he and the chiefs received their "father's" reprimands with docility, and with pleasure adopted the means that their "father" proposed to them to repair their faults, and thanked him for his kindness in offering himself to be their intercessor. They were ready to do everything their "father" commanded them to do.

Such is the sense (if the terms are not quite the same) of the response that Mechtechiko made in the name of the chiefs and The Mortar.

I will always remember the evidence of joy that Colonel Wedderburn showed at the sight of the savages' docility, and the evidence of their confidence and friendship which they gave me. The Colonel, in a transport of joy, asked me to negotiate an adoption of brotherhood between himself and The Mortar. On my proposing this to the chief, he said that he would adopt his "father's" friend as a brother with pleasure; then, addressing himself to the Colonel, he said to him, "You are a war-chief; I am also. When two war-chiefs adopt one another as brothers, they should always be ready to give mutual aid; you may have need of me; I may have need of you; we ought not fail one another on such occasions."

The Colonel, delighted by that response, displayed his affection in terms which manifested the noble manner of his thinking, and as evidence of the sincerity of his expressions, he offered to be intercessor, as well as I, for the pardon which I should ask of

Messrs. Johnstone and Stuart for the Creek Nation; and all the chiefs and warriors shouted their applause at that proposition. Colonel Wedderburn, then, as well as I, was an actor in the comedy which we put on. This, the prologue of the piece, will instruct by its contents.

I have already spoken of the murder committed by the Tallapoosas; of the Indians' deputation; of their sentiments toward the English; of the project which I formed of engaging them to present themselves, if not in an altogether humble posture, at least decently; of the reprimand that I made to the savages; I have said that, as means of repairing their fault, I proposed to place myself at their head to intercede for their pardon; of their acceptance of my intercession and Colonel Wedderburn's.

After having received the savages' word and having concerted the maneuvers that we would make with them, the Colonel and I returned to Pensacola carrying the good news to Messrs. Johnstone and Stuart who were delighted at the Indians' good disposition but, I believe, were forming additional jealousy against me.

Our agreements with the savages were that, as soon as we saw them approaching the town, the Colonel and I would go place ourselves at their head at the bank of a brook which runs about half a mile from the fort at Pensacola, whither the Colonel and I betook ourselves as soon as we were told that the Indians appeared to be advancing toward the town. We were most surprised to learn from the interpreter that the savages had stopped a half-mile from the creek and demanded that Messrs. Johnstone and Stuart be there to receive them and place themselves at their head for purposes of entering the town. Chagrined and justly irritated by such a change, I sent several interpreters to reproach them for their irresolution; their messages were in vain; the Indians were resolved that nothing should turn them away from what they asked. I saw myself on the verge of admitting that I had no influence over their minds. I sent my son with instructions to say to The Mortar that I awaited him, that I was surprised at his change, and that I had never known him to be a man to fail of his word. As soon as The Mortar saw my son, he held out his hand to him. My son having told him that I awaited him, he got up, without giving him time to finish what he had to say, and himself said to his people, "Let us go join our 'father,' who awaits us at the bank of the stream." The junction being made, The Mortar took us, the Colonel and me, each by the arm; two other of the most outstanding chiefs took our other two arms, and thus we set out toward the fort, having behind us all the greatest chiefs, followed by the war-chiefs and warriors who were chanting peaceful songs and dancing peace dances. Having arrived at Mr. Johnstone's gate, the dances and songs ceased; we presented ourselves at the dwelling where Messrs. Johnstone, Stuart, Admiral Sir William Burnaby, all the notables of the law, the military, the church, commerce, &c. awaited us. The apartment was so full that we, the Colonel, myself, and the Indians, would have had some trouble in entering if we had not been the actors in the comedy which was being played, for it is thus that Governor Johnstone characterizes that business so humiliating to the savages. Being thus arrived, the Colonel and I, each holding a symbolic spotless white eagle-tail fan in our hands, advanced towards Mr. Johnstone, the Admiral, and Stuart. I delivered the "talk" to Mr. Johnstone first, approximately in these terms:

"There, Sir, are folk who would be willing to call you their father, but as yet they see you only as their judge, to whom they come asking pardon as criminals. They beg you, Sir, to consider that the real culprits are not within their control, and as they are in an impossible situation to give the English the satisfaction which is due, they adjure you not to make the entire Nation miserable by punishing the innocent for a crime committed by certain private individuals without the approbation of their Nation.

"These people have chosen the Colonel and me as their intercessors before you; they have placed in our hands these signs of the candor of their sentiments. The Colonel and I implore you to make this day happy by accepting the peaceful tokens which we present you in behalf of the suppliants."

Mr. Johnstone having accepted the white eagle-tail which I held, the savages made the assembly-place resound with a sort of grunting which expressed their joy. The Colonel gave the white eagle-tail which he held to Mr. Johnstone: I carried mine to Mr.

Stuart, to whom I made the same discourse as to Mr. Johnstone, adding (as I knew him to be punctilious about precedence) that I had addressed the "talk" to Mr. Johnstone first because I envisaged the affair as regarding him directly, having occurred in his Province, but that he could be assured that on every occasion I would render to him that which I owed him, recognizing that I depended on him more than anyone.

If an affair of that kind can be termed (as Mr. Johnstone says) a mock comedy, all the reparations which are made by nation to nation, by individual to individual, by family to family, could be so termed; in this case, the kings, individuals, and heads of family would be wrong to wish to humiliate their enemies—every act of humility being termed derisive in the opinion of Mr. Johnstone, who, however, I believe will find few followers of his way of thinking.

That ceremony finished, all the Indians came to shake hands with the Governor, Superintendent, the Admiral and the most notable men of the assembly, and each having taken his place, Mr. Johnstone made a little speech to the Indians in which he announced his decision to pardon them and the satisfaction he had of seeing them in such a good mood. The Indians spoke in their turn; I will speak only concerning what they said that related to me.

I summon here all the English then resident in Pensacola. I am sure there is not one who would not deny Mr. Johnstone's charge, and who would only bear out The Mortar and all the other chiefs who spoke, affirming that of all the invitations which had been made to them, they had acceded only to mine, carried by my son. There was not one who had not spoken of me several times over as "father" and testified great satisfaction at seeing their "father" again. Does Mr. Johnstone dare say, without fear of encountering a thousand contradictions, that Mr. Struthers' name alone was mentioned in that conference or in the following, except as far as it was put forward by Mr. Stuart in asking the savages if they were willing to accept him as commissary in their Nation. The congress was almost finished when that proposition was made.

Several days passed in conferences before concluding the treaty.

As long as my health permitted, I assisted at the conferences, and Mr. Johnstone cannot deny, without lying, that while I was present, The Mortar and Mechtechiko, who were those who harangued the most often, pronounced not a single speech without speaking advantageously of me, of the confidence that they had in me, and that it was only at my persuasion that they were present at the congress and disposed to contract an alliance with the English. Finally my illness grew worse. I was obliged to keep to my chamber and even to my bed. The savages being much opposed to the land concessions, I asked Colonel Wedderburn to consent again to explain to the interpreters a little speech which I wanted to make to The Mortar and a half a score of the other most honored chiefs, in order that they might win over their warriors' minds to the point on which I wished to speak to them, which was to make a generous cession of their lands, following a straight line prolonging the limits fixed by the Choctaws. I found more difficulty in gaining that point than I had ever found in all the negotiations I have conducted with those Nations. They were resolved to confine the English in very narrow bounds, and as Mr. Johnstone and Stuart said, if I had not been in the English interest, and if I had been absent from the congress, in all probability the limits of the cession would not have been so extensive. I was heard to hold the following discourse several times:

"Is it possible (the chiefs said to me) that you, who at the time you were with the French so often exhorted us not to yield a bit of land to the English, you chide us today, and press us with so much fluency to give it up to them?"

To this I replied: "Never having spoken except in your interests, without asking anything of you for myself, I am still the same toward you as I have always been, giving you my counsel as a father for your well-being. When I forbade your giving land to the English, the French and they were at war. If the English had come to make a settlement near the French, there would have been fighting, the one against the other; some of you would have taken the part of the English, others that of the French; brother would have perished at the hand of brother; son, perhaps, would have killed father, &c. Finally you would have endured all the horrors of a civil war. Today, not only are the French and English friends, but the King of France has even ceded his claims over lands including your Nations to the English. Wherever you turn you will encounter the English. If you refuse them land which they can sow, you withhold from them the means of furnishing you sustenance when you come to them in great number; thus, far from calling you to them, they will put you off as much as they can, and consequently, you deprive yourselves of all annual or occasional gifts."

By such discourses I determined them to restrict the English in less narrow confines; and Messrs. Johnstone and Stuart could not deny, I believe, that it was in my room that the limits were drawn of the land cession which the savages made, which satisfied Messrs. Johnstone and Stuart and all the English who were then in Pensacola. It was only I who reproached the savages with the fact that they were letting themselves be surpassed in generosity by the Choctaws, who had fixed their boundaries more distant than they.

To this they replied that perhaps one day they would be more generous than the Choctaws, that they wished to execute the terms of the treaty which they were about to make in good faith, that therefore they had reserved a part of the land which they might cede after they knew the English better, that if, after having passed some years with them, they found them good, they would cede as much land as they might need.

If, following the savages' lessons, I had put the English in the position of always having need of my services, Mr. Johnstone would not have dared to pronounce a charge so full of iniquity against me, but, full of sentiments of honor, I have, with good faith, rendered all the services it was in my power to render. Mr. Johnstone, who hoped not to succeed, and by the means of a war that he considered declaring, hoped to make immense profits on the expenditures which would have been made at his direction, seeing his prize escape him, has sated his vengeance on the person who, by faithful service, smoothed all the difficulties. I say this because Mr. Johnstone told me several times that his greatest interest could be realized by great trouble in the Province subject to his command;

he would work against himself by bringing it to a state of peacefulness in good faith.

I could only laud a manner of thinking which would have been very noble, if the sentiments had conformed to the words. Then, I did not know the fate that threatened me, and I could scarcely believe that Mr. Johnstone would behave with extreme violence toward me in hope only of exciting the murmurs of the Nations and bringing them to a war which would give him the means of amassing great wealth.

The savages' resolution on the limits of the land being taken, Messrs. Stuart and Johnstone being satisfied by the cession which the Indians were to make to the English, I was absent from all affairs in order to apply myself solely to my convalescence. Messrs. Johnstone and Stuart concerted with the savages the day on which the treaty was to be signed, and I do not know for what reason they adopted the—according to me, indecorous—course of going into the woods to conclude a treaty that would have been the more glorious for being completed on the spot; and they ought to have been even more careful not to engage themselves in that business (which degraded their character) which the savages tried to demand from the first day, and which I (as I have shown) opposed. If Messrs. Johnstone's and Stuart's intention was to conclude the treaty in the woods, they ought to have held all the conferences there; if they only conceded to the savages' too haughty petition, I think that they were wrong.

Be that as it may, the treaty was concluded in the woods; no one informed me of it. Immediately upon signing, the savages said that since they had granted the English all that had been asked, they hoped that a request which they had to make—that the English would postpone hearing what the savages had to say until after dinner—would not be refused them (this is how the matter was reported to me, for I was not present there). Upon Messrs. Stuart's and Johnstone's return from the woods, they dined with the savages, and I did not see a single one of them all that day. Dinner finished, Messrs. Johnstone and Stuart entered in conference with the savages. The Mortar, in the name of his Nation, demanded that they make it a regulation for the traders who were with the Tallapoosas, Cowetas, Abihkas, Alabamas, &c., that they sell merchandise at the same price as the traders among the Cherokees sell in that Nation. The Mortar happened to have been with the Cherokees where he had seen for himself that which was the object of his demand. Thus he could not be mistaken.

I do not know exactly what Messrs. Stuart's and Johnstone's reply was; it was so unsatisfactory to the Indians that they immediately returned to their camp where they held council. They sent word to Messrs. Stuart and Johnstone that it was necessary to tear up the treaty or burn it, that they were resolved to leave, not even desiring to receive any presents from the English.

I do not know when that response was carried to Messrs. Johnstone and Stuart; I only learned of it the next day from them, and they supplied me with the chief's demands.

In spite of the illness that I suffered, I dressed myself and betook myself to the place where the conference was being held. I found Mr. Johnstone haranguing his best to explain to the Indians that it was not dependent upon Mr. Stuart nor on him to make a reduction of the trade rates without being authorized to do so by action emanating from an authority superior to theirs. As soon as I entered, Mr. Johnstone said to the Indians, "You have confidence in M. de Monberaut; ask him if it is in my power to grant you your demand." Then neither Mr. Johnstonc nor Stuart said that I was the instigator or subduer of the troubles that they had with the savages, for Mr. Stuart, near whom I was placed, took great care to interpret to me the reference that Mr. Johnstone had just made to the Indians concerning me; upon which I said to Mr. Stuart that, if he judged it proper, I would speak to the savages myself. Having explained to him very carefully the form that I wished to give to my little exhortation, not only did he find it suitable, but he even urged Mr. Johnstone to abridge his speech in order that I might speak as soon as possible.

Here is roughly the *précis* of my discourse to the savages, which was explained to the interpreter by Colonel Wedderburn.

"Since the moment of your arrival until now, my children, I have received only cause for satisfaction from you. With pleasure I saw the negotiations between you and the English terminating without a contest; a request was no sooner made than it was granted.

"At the very moment when I believed everything generally decided, I saw you literally afflicted—about to break off because they refused to grant you a bagatelle which is not essential to your well-being. You have formerly paid for merchandise much more dearly than you pay for it today! In spite of that costliness, you sustain your wives and your children, with trouble, certainly, but you do not succumb under the burden. You believe yourselves at the zenith of good fortune when a price-reduction is accorded you, and the tariff is regulated to the price at which you pay for merchandise today—on which you demand that they make a new reduction which does not depend on the chiefs of whom you demand it! That I swear to you truthfully. These chiefs promise to write in your behalf to the common father of the red men and the white men, King George. Moreover, you can rely upon the word that they give you, for you have proof that in all the demands that you have made, when it was in their power to grant them to you, they have not refused you anything. You have testified to putting your confidence in me; you are right; I have never failed you; I will not fail you today. Give me evidence of your friendship by rendering yourselves amenable to the exhortation that I make you. Let the treaty remain, and have confidence in the good will that your fathers, the English, show you."

After I had finished speaking, Mr. Stuart made an exhortation to the Indians.

The Mortar made the replies, for he spoke to us one after the other. I will say nothing of what he said to Messrs. Johnstone and Stuart, but here is the *précis* of what he said to me. As Mr. Wedderburn had left the assembly-place on some business which called him, only Mr. Stuart, the Superintendent, and Charles Stuart, his nephew, explained to me what the interpreters were saying that The Mortar said to me. This is nothing secret; it occurred in public before all the notables of Pensacola, whom I claim for witnesses.

"I have been invited from several places to go to hear 'talks.' I did not wish to go anywhere. My father over there* finally sent a writ-

* M. de Monberaut.

ten 'talk' which was carried to me by his son. He invited me to go hear yet other words which he and the English chiefs had to say to me. I have been raised as a child cherished on my father's knees,* to whom I have never lied, and he will judge, himself, that the words which I am going to give him are not lies. I did not come here to grieve my father.† Thus, I believe, since he tells me, that it is not in the English chiefs' power to grant me my demands. There (showing the portrait of the King) is the father of all the red men and white men. These chiefs assure me that they are going to write to him, to the end that they will give us merchandise at a better price. I believe that, since my father assures me of it. I am going to exhort my warriors to have patience until they have received the reply of the great chief of all the English.

"I also ask my father, M. de Monberaut, to say to the English chief that he ought not be aroused against me because I uphold the interests of my people. He says that he is the father of his; I am of mine!"

The details which I have to present may be boring because of their length. I certainly wish I were able to abridge them, but it is essential to me to display things that have happened in a true-to-life manner. Having said nothing other than the truth, in which I am certain not to be contradicted by any of the attendants at the congress, I shall observe that Mr. Johnstone accuses me wrongfully of having been the author and queller of difficulties made by the savages, &c. And if Mr. Johnstone spoke the truth, he could say without error that he had not recognized the evil in his own antechamber! Why, in front of everybody, did he appear to be so much upset by the savages' resolution?

I will ask my illustrious judges yet again to be permitted to put before their eyes an observation which the distance of circumstances and their great embarrassment might cause them to omit.

Great God! but the difference between an honorable man and a perfidious one is enormous! The perfidious man wishes unceasingly to appropriate the honor and the property of the other. The man of honor, on the contrary, not only gives to each his due, but even

* The same M. de Monberaut.

† The same.

seeks the means of throwing luster on the actions of persons under his orders.

I beg His Excellency General Gage to permit me to use his name in contrast to those of Mr. Johnstone and Stuart!

His Excellency, in accounting to the English ministry the means that he employed for the reduction of the savages, quite sure that they will always attribute to the head the glory of the blows that it has suggested to the arm to carry out, did not forget to render Colonel Bouquet's actions illustrious. I beg His Excellency again to permit me to transcribe here the terms which he inserted in his letter to the ministry dated December 13, 1764:

> and in justice to Col. Bouquet, I must testify the obligations I have to him and that nothing, but the firm and steady conduct which he has observed in all his transactions with those treacherous savages would ever have brought them to a serious peace.*

Why, Messrs. Johnstone and Stuart, have you not followed so good an example which could not be unknown to you? It was with you that, for the first time, I read the journal in which that letter of His Excellency General Gage is cited in its entirety—at whose observations jealousy possessed itself of your hearts. Can anyone be ignorant of your qualities, the one Governor of the Province, and the other Superintendent for the savages, to whom I am only the deputy? Could there have been anyone in the world who would not know that I could do no good except in your behalf? I could only give to the savages hopes of the benefits which were at your disposal. Have I not told the savages that it was from your hands that I held an employment which allowed me to continue to serve them as father? If you have forgotten that I so instructed the savages, re-read my harangues, and you will see that they are full of evidence which will prove it.

Why, then, since you cannot doubt that the little glory which I might acquire would revert to you, have you (with a perfidy more condemnable than that of assassins who only threaten life) sought to appropriate my property by depriving me of my honor? You have deceived yourselves, however; liars and calumniators that you are,

* Page 52 of the book entitled *The Universal Magazine* for January 1765.

it will be impossible for you to tarnish the reputation of a man, all of whose actions have been directed by sentiments of probity and the purest honor. You have ruined and humiliated me, but you cannot dishonor me; my triumph will be more considerable when your characters shall be perfectly known!

Arts. 12, 13, and 14—The course of this memorial is already too long and boring, though true. I have given so many proofs of Mr. Johnstone's perfidy and his naive imposture, that I could leave all the rest of his letter without reply; so, I only wish to answer the following articles most succinctly.

If I had not accepted employment, not having taken the oath as a subject, I would not, in any fashion, have been obliged (even if, indeed, I should have remained in English territory) to make any effort to conciliate the savages to the British government; but having gone so far as to accept a commission, I contracted obligations which I have executed with honor, and Mr. Johnstone dishonors himself by adding to the impostures with which his iniquitous arrêt is filled, the ironic trait of saying that he will see "how far my authority with the chiefs will prevail when situated in another country where there are no English presents; it will be proven, &c."

Without nourishing myself on such foolish ideas as Mr. Johnstone—who, beyond desiring to have the crowns of France, Spain and England for enemies, here evokes the spirit of Ajax in order to make him see the light of day, &c.—ingenuously avowing my slight power before such personages or nations as have power, and hoping for some royal gratification, I shall answer him that if, as he, I were depository and master of gratifications in the name of a king, if I had an antagonist like Mr. Johnstone, who is only arrogant in prosperity, as I have proved him to be, I would find him scarcely redoubtable, especially at present, as I have certain knowledge of his natural greediness.

As to his saying that "the alteration of circumstances will not make any impression or alteration in his conduct, &c."—The sort of iniquitous authority that he has exercised over me proves that he has none of the integrity that he wants to appear to have. As long as he had need of me, he caressed me, showed me respect which he did not owe me, and made me promises which probably exceeded his authority, and, to give some color to the disloyalty of his action, he says that my character, perfectly known, has put him in the position of adopting a manner toward me so little in keeping with the services that I have rendered. He could not keep from avowing, however, that he is the only one who thinks that my services are useless. He indicates to me, himself, that I had misunderstood his intentions by not resigning the commission that I had received from Mr. Stuart and himself, and which they probably had only given me knowing their own insufficiency to lead the savages to the point that they desired, and in that case (he says), I would have been right, according to the conventions or stipulations which I had made; and in order to screen me from the blame which he well foresaw could scarcely be attributed to him for his breach of faith, he was not ashamed to agree to being taxed with incapacity, provided that he could accuse me of having practiced the arts of subtlety. However, he has had time to notice the said traits of subtlety, since he only sent me his letter consenting to all my propositions more than three weeks after I had sent the letter containing the articles of agreement which I wished to make to him and to Mr. Stuart. The said letter was, further, communicated to him before a fair copy was made, and there was no expression nor proposition in it which Messrs. Johnstone and Stuart had not approved and promised to ratify before my letter had been delivered to them. Why should Mr. Johnstone and Stuart's response be dated December 15, 1764? It was only sent back to me on January 8, 1765, the day on which they sent me my commission, although I performed the function more than three weeks earlier. This was the first fraud which Mr. Stuart perpetrated, which ought to have prepared me for receiving others from him.

What has happened to Mr. Johnstone's insight not to remark that I would employ traits of subtlety? He is incapable or deceitful, although I have not put any sort of subtlety to practice, and as all my actions have been directed by candor and good faith, I can declare without fear of contradiction that he is both the one and the other; and unfortunate is the province, and unfortunate are the people exposed to the iniquitous traits of which Mr. George Johnstone is capable, who himself, uniquely capable of employing such subtle traits, wishes to render the suit which I made to Mr. Stuart and him culpable, by telling me openly that the profession of the Catholic religion which I make is incompatible with the exercise of my employment.

I swear that that question ought to appear humiliating to him! It proves to him, as I perceive it, that Mr. Stuart and he have employed the most subtle means to engage me to furnish them my aid in order to conclude the peace with the savages, and that promptly after the conclusion of that peace and alliance, they sought only to find some means of excluding me from an employment that they had assured me would not be incompatible with my religious profession, the creation being posterior to the laws relative to the subject of religion. It is correct to say that General Gage's letter ought not have left me in any doubt on that subject, and I ask His Excellency General Gage to accept my excuses for having thought too lightly of the faith of a governor and a superintendent, as the observation has escaped him that an employment created posterior to the law on the subject of religion could but be subject to the said law.

"With respect (Mr. Johnstone continues) to the articles of capitulation, they could not be stronger if I were to sign them a thousand times; they will always remain as the first treaties made, and I deny that they are in any measure correspondent to those which you have stated; I think you have acted nine days, and you demand an annual pension as large as the full pay you received from the King of France; the important points have been left to the ministry to determine, following the agreements, &c."

Before replying to that article, I shall say that Mr. Johnstone employs a culpable indecency by comparing the entire revenue of the King of France with the demand I made of a pension of 105 pounds sterling.

He says that he denies the articles of agreement whose execution I demand.

The letter in which my propositions, and Messrs. Johnstone and Stuart's acceptance without reservation whatever, are contained, is at the head of this memorial; thus our illustrious judges may see whether he or I be false in his charges. He says that he believed

I had served nine days, &c. He calculates badly; he had only to see the date of the commission that Mr. Stuart and he had given me and compare it with that of his letter full of calumnies, but even if I had only served one day, that day having been glorious and advantageous to Great Britain, I ought not expect the perfidious darts which Mr. Johnstone hurls at me. A single day of service as essential as that which I rendered should merit a pension as large and larger than that which I ask—which is owed me. The terms of my agreement on that subject are express. When I made that demand I would never have suspected Messrs. Johnstone and Stuart capable of using perfidy. I fear that some individual, jealous of seeing me occupy an employment which he thought he merited, has sent a disadvantageous portrayal of my person and my talents to the ministry; moreover (I hoped, in truth, to succeed in my enterprise, but) having to deal with savages, it might have chanced that I would have run aground. The ministry, forewarned by that which had been indicated to it, and seeing the hopes which had been given it become vain, could not have approved Messrs. Johnstone and Stuart's choice. Therefore I wish to be indemnified for the sacrifices that I made, but as I have succeeded and as my greatest persecutors are Messrs. Johnstone and Stuart, who sought after me with inconceivable earnestness, and who have become my enemies only because they wish to appropriate the glory which is due me, I have recourse to the authority of the King and his ministers, not only to allow me the pension which is due me, but even to make reparations for my honor and indemnities for my possessions &c.

The rest of that paragraph of Mr. Johnstone's letter is a repetition of his famous arrêt, made with all possible iniquity and against the law of the kingdom. I refer for my response to what I have said above.

The 15th and 16th Articles of the same letter are also a repetition of injuries which he has spoken against me, and of the advice that he had given Mr. Stuart of awaiting the ministry's decision in my case &c.

I have, in the course of this memorial, given so many proofs of the fidelity with which I have served, and of Mr. Johnstone's perfidy, that it would be mere wantonness to bore the reader, if I made a particular reply to the two articles above mentioned. All who know, be it ever so little, the character of Mr. Johnstone, know that that man is a hundred times more the enemy of the king and the state than those who daily plot revolution.

Art. 17 "Since you have heard that your goods in New Orleans are in danger, the sooner you go there to save them, the better it will be. I hope that there is as little foundation in that report as in the letter you have shown me & caused to be seen, in which it is noted that Mr. Aubry had detained your Croix de St. Louis &c. If the King of England is to pay for your effects, I have no doubt that they will be condemned and amount to a pretty large sum."

I have at hand a letter from Mr. Petit who indicates to me that the goods of persons who expatriate themselves, being subject to being seized by the crown, it could happen that a suit moved between my son-in-law and my son, with whom I hold a common property, could well be cause that mine would be confiscated. Consequently, I wrote to Messrs. Johnstone and Stuart that my goods were being prosecuted. I could be in the position of going to New Orleans myself to endeavor to put my goods in surety. Mr. Johnstone takes occasion from that article of my letter to say offensive things about me and to tell a lie—if not in fact, at least under the circumstances.

Necessarily, in all his charges, there must always be something of falsehood, for I have never shown him any letter in which it was affirmatively stated that Mr. Aubry had held up my Croix de St. Louis. How would he be able to detain it? He does not have it, and he has not received it yet. The letter that I had shown him was from my son-in-law, who showed his anxiety for my making up my mind to remain in a foreign land, and especially for what I had written to Mr. Aubry, that I would serve the King of England with the same zeal, with the same fidelity and with the same sentiments of honor and probity with which I have formerly served the King of France. He said to me, conjecturally, that these sentiments expressed by me placed Mr. Aubry in the position of not sending me the Croix de St. Louis which I was to have received, my brother having told him that I was nominated for it several years ago. Colonel Wedderburn, who was present when I showed that letter to Mr. Johnstone and who has also seen the letter of explanation which I have written on that subject to Mr. Aubry, can certify that it was not a question of Mr. Aubry's effectively holding back my Croix de St. Louis, but of being in a position to retain it if it were sent to him. Thus, as may be seen, I do not wrongfully accuse Mr. Johnstone of being fallacious in his charges. This is another paragraph which will prove his slanderous humor.

"I have also had," he says, "some trouble in getting your son out of a vexatious prosecution as a horse-thief, but as I suppose he imagined himself still in the Indian Nation, he had not that turpitude of intention which the law supposes to accompany such an action, &c."

In order to show how great Mr. Johnstone's malice is, for full answer to that article I shall transcribe a letter from Mr. Noble to my son which will prove that my son has not stolen the horse which Mr. Johnstone mentions, and in order not to bore the reader, I will pass over Mr. Johnstone's maneuvers on that subject which do not honor him.

Copy of the letter of Mr. Noble, Merchant at Pensacola, to the son of M. de Monberaut.

Pensacola, 6th July 1765

SIR:

I have the honor of receiving your favor of the 28th ult. by which I see that you are inquiet on the subject of the horse which you have taken here with my consent. I will tell you that the day after your departure, I immediately arranged with the person to whom he belonged, etc. I beg you not to regard what everyone says, since it is already a closed affair as much on my part as that of Mr. Gerome. I offer you my most sincere services, also to Monsieur, your dear father, to whom I beg you to say that I shall always be charmed to give him evidence of my friendship. I am, with the utmost esteem,

Sir, your most humble and most obedient servant,
Signed James Noble

I would certainly have preferred not to make all of Mr. Johnstone's iniquity public. I would even have been able to think that he had only been carried to such extremities because he had let himself be taken in by some false report, but the end of his letter leaves me no doubt about his sentiments. I would have taken the trouble of writing to him, and, appropriately, of making him reconsider his prejudices, if he had not written to me himself.

"I have nothing further of use to add than to assure you this is my final resolution on your subject, and therefore you cannot hope that I shall employ any more time in answering any memorial which might be sent hereafter. I am, &c."

Being thus able to hope for nothing on Mr. Johnstone's part, I have recourse to the supreme authority, begging His Britannic Majesty or his ministers to tender me a helping hand, to make my innocence, oppressed by the most iniquitous of all men, triumph.

It is to the interest of the government and the good name of the English to provide me the means of justification and to procure me the reparation due my honor, for if on this occasion Mr. Johnstone's perfidy finds any support, and if he is not punished for his iniquity, no one can say that in England faithful and useful service is recompensed, it being noted that the zealous servant who discharges it with honor is loaded with infamy. This cannot happen under the reign of King George whom, with just reason, Europe recognizes as a monarch most just and magnanimous, for whose preservation and prosperity I shall not cease to address my prayers to Heaven.

I certify that the copies of letters transcribed at the head of this memorial, after the preface, two others from Mr. Stuart transcribed in the body of the memorial, and one from Mr. Noble, transcribed at the end of the said memorial, are taken word for word from the originals which are in my hands, without there being anything changed, added, or taken away; in evidence of which I have initialed all the leaves of the memorial M M^{t}.

I further attest and here take my most binding oath, that all the justifying evidence which I have set down in my memorial is exactly true, and that the imputations that Mr. Johnstone has made against me are calumnies.

At New Orleans this
1st February 1766

The Chevalier Montault de Monberaut

Index